I Have Waited for You:

Letters from Prison

ASHLEY ASTI

ISBN: 9781718122727

"The best way to support an oppressed people
is to not speak over
or in place of them."
—Khaled Beydoun

D1399927

ASHLEY ASTI

Anthony Bourdain said it about travel,
but the essence is the same.
I'm going to say it like this:

Connecting with people who, at first, seem so
unlike yourself "isn't always pretty. It isn't always
comfortable. Sometimes, it hurts, it even breaks
your heart. But that's okay. The journey changes
you; it should change you...You take something
with you. Hopefully, you leave something good
behind."

ASHLEY ASTI

CONTENTS

INTRODUCTION

This is not a book about prison.

This is a book about human beings.

About connection. About seeing and being seen.

About kindness and redemption and what draws us together; this is a book about hope.

This is a book about change.

And, mostly, this is a book about love.

This book is not a statement against mass incarceration because it overtly addresses the *in*justice system, but because the human beings who happen to be incarcerated who speak within it are, in themselves—in their humanity —bold testimonies against it.

The book's title—*I Have Waited for You*—is accurate because this book is also about waiting. Waiting for freedom and waiting for each other.

It's about the anticipation of receiving a letter (Eric, in Chapter Five, uses the phrase "wag," like a dog wagging his tail, to describe the feeling). It's about the joy, too often lost now, of knowing someone took the time to sit down and write, thinking only of you—and the magic of dropping these letters in the mail and having them take their own unknowable journeys across the country to wind up, somehow, in your hands. It's about surprise.

And it's about holding the paper someone else held and seeing the ink, set down in someone else's handwriting, on the page and feeling, for just a moment, closer. Like maybe you know them better now.

It's about the anger and frustration of waiting for minds to change and policies to change like dominoes, one propelling the other.

And it's about belief, about waiting for the fruits of your faith to manifest, hoping and trusting that they will.

But the book's title doesn't really come from any of those modes of waiting. It comes from a letter sent to me by Ernest L. Young, Sr., whose letters are in Chapter Eleven. "I have waited for you," he told me. But, if I have spoken truthfully, I have waited for them, too.

I set out on a mission to honor the voices of people who are incarcerated. "Share your voice," I asked them, and I sent them a list of questions about themselves which became the launching point for this book. I wanted to let them know I see them, I hear them, and that I think you should see and hear them, too.

Because we cannot create change by disappearing people. We're wasting away so much talent. We're locking up moms and dads which means we're not locking them up alone; their children feel the bars, too. We're locking up artists and writers and friends; teachers and leaders. Co-creators. People who need and deserve healing.

Want to see a community thriving? Watch the way it grows its people, knowing no one is too lost. It does not give up on anyone.

So I wanted to see and to show. But I have fallen for my own trick: when humanity rises, in this case from the page of a letter, it is not there merely to be seen and shown: it sees you, too.

What I have received in return for this project has changed me. I feel like I am a sprouting seed and each of these people I have corresponded with—whether we have written each other one letter or twenty-five—has walked alongside me, paused, and watered me.

To each of you who has taken the time to see me, too, I thank you. You have trusted me with your voices and I have trusted you with mine, and I didn't know that this is what I was seeking—the world-opening power of connection.

I have waited for this and I have waited for you.

So, yes, mostly, this book is about love.

ASHLEY ASTI

ACKNOWLEDGEMENTS

My name is on this book, but it is not mine alone. It is a co-creation, shaped by twelve individuals who are incarcerated whose voices are in this book, and nine others who have written to me or continue to write to me whose words have contributed to this book in spirit. This book is because of each of you.

I want to thank Melissa Bee and her brother Rick, whose work at Adopt an Inmate is the bedrock upon which this book stands. At mail call, many inmates never hear their name called. Melissa and Rick have shown that, "with pen, paper, and stamps, you can change that"—and it can change you.

And then there is Bryan Stevenson. I've never met him, but his integrity and purpose rise, unmissable, through his book. Reading *Just Mercy* was my first taste of the entrenched and intertwined woes of mass incarceration, poverty, inequality, and race and it woke me up, although there is always more waking up to do. "When you experience mercy," he wrote, whether you're showing it or receiving it, "you learn things that are hard to learn otherwise. You see things you can't otherwise see; you hear things you can't otherwise hear. You begin to recognize the humanity that resides in each of us." I have merely tasted mercy while writing this book and it feels like seeing from the other side of the moon, full of contradictions and blessings. And, somehow, it feels like oneness.

To my sisters-in-spirit, Alicia and Britney, the first two women who happen to be incarcerated who I began writing with over two years ago—thank you. Britney, when you write to me and call me your sister, it humbles me. You are a survivor. A fighter. A warrioress. Even after the throes of nearly five years of solitary confinement, you wrote to me, "I've learned that no matter what, no matter where I am, no matter when, God never leaves me or forsakes me. I must give to those in need. Somewhere, someone needs a hug or an ear to listen or a shoulder to lean on. I can give that."

And, Alicia, you feel like what a sister should, listening, caring, and offering advice about life and about men. You remind me of my purpose and to hold my head up even when I can't see far in front of me. Your words are still pinned above my desk: "I urge you to continue your work and reaching out to others because someone is always listening. The days you don't feel like it are the days you have to strive the most." Thank you for the privilege of your friendship.

I want to thank Gin, who connected me with Taj, for her kindness, for sharing a meal and sharing an extra reusable fork with me to spare the planet from gratuitous plastic waste, and for her unmistakeable blue hair that makes smiles contagious.

And then there are the others, the spirit helpers, whose presence—physical or spiritual—have carried me through. There are too many to list, so, here, I will celebrate just two: Alice Walker and, most especially, my mom.

In no particular order, the friends in prisons across the country whose words may not appear in this book, but whose contributions can be felt and deserve to be known:

Christine
Latif
Robert F.
Elsie
Alicia
Britney
April
Brittany
Davieon

Angela

One.

May 14, 2018

1. Introduce yourself! Tell me a little about you:

My name is Angela Rocka. I am a lady of 48, blue eyed, blonde hair, at 5 foot and 137 lbs. I love surfing, animals, reading, and all outdoor activities. I am single and I love making people laugh.

2. Describe what you look like. What do you like about how you look? Is there something you wish you could change?

I have tan skin, athletic, with a wild white streak in the front of my hair. The most I love about my looks are my eyes. I have fox eyes, I'm told.

What would I change about me? My height.

3. Do you have family? If so, tell me about them.

I do have parents, yet I am adopted so I do not know who my family is. I have three beautiful kids who are 23, 25, and 26.

4. Do you have children? If so, what do you most love about them? What do you miss about them?

What I love most about my kids are they each have different personalities, yet they're all like mine. I miss sleeping with them and doing schoolwork with them.

5. What are your goals?

My goals are to earn a surf shop that I can run by myself, yet I also want to help the elderly and take in animals with no homes.

6. If you could leave prison for a day, what would you do?

If I could leave prison for one day, I'd go spend it with my parents and kids. I've been locked up since 2000.

7. Do you believe your life has a purpose or specific mission? What is it?

Yes. Yet I'm not sure what it is yet. I try to teach the younger generation as much positivity as I can.

8. What do you think makes a good friend?

Loyalty makes a good friend.

9. What's your biggest life lesson so far?

My biggest life lesson is that family comes before anything—before money, drugs, or men.

10. What advice would you give to your younger self or to a child in a similar position as you were when you were young?

Sticks and stones…don't worry about what people say about you.

11. What does it feel like to live in prison?

I feel like a caged, angry bird, that my wings are broken.

12. How do you feel about the prison system or the justice system?

I am in prison with DNA to clear me of my crime, but I don't have the funds to fight my case. The justice system is a disgrace, unjustified, and only a money-making system.

13. What makes you laugh?

Babies and animals make me laugh.

14. Finish the sentence:
If I could change the world, I would get rid of racism.

I believe all kids of color should play together without embarrassment or repercussions.

I wish there was no such thing as bullying.

I am inspired by nothing anymore simply because I am stuck in prison.

15. Please share anything else you'd like. This is your space. And your voice.

Thank you for the opportunity to speak my voice. I have a good testimony for you if you ever just wanna talk. I've done 18 in a 60 year sentence for wrongful conviction. I was 29 when I got locked up. The only thing about being here so long is I *still* look 29! Yup, prison preserved me.

I'm still fighting my case. I will *not* give up. It's people like you who shows people like me I am not forgotten. Thank you.

Thank you for your time,
Angela Rocka

May 28, 2018

Angela,

I am so grateful that my friend Britney spread the "Share Your Voice" questions to you. She is a woman unafraid of her power and her voice and I can tell that you are powerful, too.

At the end of your letter to me, you wrote and underlined, "It's people like you who shows people like me I'm not forgotten." If there's anything I can offer you, it's that I hear you and I see you (through eyes beyond the physical) and that, I am certain, you matter.

But, more than that, I want to thank you. Your words bring you to life in my eyes. Your words remind me that millions of others with voices and stories and talents of their own remain locked up behind bars across this country. Your words teach me compassion and reaffirm the knowing we have somehow shoved down and too often forgotten that we are one, we are connected. Thank you for being my guide and teacher in this way. I am moved.

You also wrote to me about living in prison: "I feel like a caged, angry bird—that my wings are broken." And your expression immediately made me think of one of my favorite poets, who was a bold, intelligent, audacious, and beautifully expressive woman of color, Maya Angelou. She wrote a book called, *I Know Why the Caged Bird Sings,* and a poem of similar title: "Caged Bird." I have included the poem at the end of this letter in case you've never read it.

7

I also assure you: your wings are not broken. I feel you in your writing. I love the way you describe yourself, that "wild white streak" in your hair like a bolt of lightning. I feel your wild feminine coming through—bold, sensual, confident, gorgeous.

And your mission to teach the younger generation positivity is purpose, indeed. We need more teachers who feel compelled by the power of positivity.

You have a powerful voice and, in you, you know this. Your birthright is to share the gifts within you. That is your freedom. So keep offering the world what you have to say, even if it's simply in a journal to yourself. Let it come out.

I heard the other day that suffering is not the absence of talents or gifts, but the failure to give out—to share and express—those gifts. And I know you've got gems in you. We all do.

Anything else you want to share with me, I'm listening.

In solidarity,
Ashley

Maya Angelou's "Caged Bird" is below:

A free bird leaps
on the back of the wind
and floats downstream
till the current ends
and dips his wing
in the orange sun rays
and dares to claim the sky.

But a bird that stalks
down his narrow cage
can seldom see through
his bars of rage
his wings are clipped and
his feet are tied
so he opens his throat to sing.

The caged bird sings
with a fearful trill
of things unknown
but longed for still
and his tune is heard
on the distant hill
for the caged bird
sings of freedom.

The free bird thinks of another breeze
and the trade winds soft through the sighing trees
and the fat worms waiting on a dawn bright lawn
and he names the sky his own

But a caged bird stands on the grave of dreams
his shadow shouts on a nightmare scream
his wings are clipped and his feet are tied
so he opens his throat to sing.

The caged bird sings
with a fearful trill
of things unknown
but longed for still
and his tune is heard
on the distant hill
for the caged bird
sings of freedom.

Taj

Two.

My connection with Taj began with an email in my inbox with this question in the subject line: "Writing to a prisoner in Virginia?"

About a week earlier, I had sent my first round of letters to people in prisons across the country, asking if they'd like to participate in this "Share Your Voice" project, I was calling it, that was still forming.

So I clicked open the email:

April 26, 2018

Hi Ashley,

My partner Taj Alexander Mahon-Haft is in a prison here in Virginia, and we think you may have tried to write to him. He got a notification that a letter from an Ashley Asti at the address that comes up with Ashley Asti was returned for being too long.

I see that you do work with women in prison? He does a lot of amazing work with prison education and different things, as he was a sociology and criminal justice professor before he went in. In any case, please let me know if you tried to write to him and if there is any message I can relay or any help I can provide you.

I hope this finds you well.
-Gin

May 1, 2018

Hi Gin,

Thank you so much for reaching out to me. It's disappointing, but not surprising, to hear that a letter could be turned away for being too long!

I did try to connect with Taj. I've copied the letter I wrote to him below. If you're able or want to pass it on, wonderful.

Warmly,
Ashley

Hi Taj,

I came across your writing first on Adopt an Inmate's blog, and then around the web. As a writer myself (and a poet), I was drawn in by the way your words sound on the tongue and by the love and connection you convey.

I have published two books of poetry, but am embarking on a new project meant to share and celebrate the voices of individuals who are incarcerated.

My purpose for writing this letter is to tell you about this book project I'd like to pursue and to invite you to join me in it.

I've been writing to several women in Texas prisons for a couple years now after I discovered Adopt an Inmate. I'm inspired by their strength, their wisdom, and am grateful for their friendships. They feel like sisters to me now. I want other people to see that: to hear the voices of those who are incarcerated. I fear that too many people who aren't directly caught in the grip of the justice system do not realize that we are locking up potential, that we don't need cages, we need support. We need to spread more love. We need more understanding. We need more community. We need to remember that we are all more alike than different. So my idea, which is still forming, is to create a book using the words and voices of those who are incarcerated.

I've enclosed a "Share Your Voice" questionnaire for you with more information. I would be honored if you want to participate and share your answers to some or all of the questions.

Whether you choose to participate or not, I am grateful that you continue to share your voice with the world through your writing.

Kind regards,
Ashley

Taj's responses to the questions:

May 26, 2018

1. Introduce yourself! Tell me a little about you.

I am a partner, father, teacher, activist, humanist, eco-warrior, and unapologetic progressive. None of these roles take precedence, but really the first two do! I've been all these things for many years, but these social bonds and loved ones have become even more important since prison. My family is the core of my identity.

Still, nothing can stop me from also working to be the change I seek in the world. I strive to provide dignity and kindness to the disenfranchised and illuminate the humanity lost to mass incarceration. I am educated in sociology and poetry. My outspoken teaching and advocacy garnered me the legal attention that allowed me this participant perspective on the system of criminal injustice. I am even more committed to reform now, with my unique intersection of roles and my heightened compassion for the deprivation and dehumanization experienced by people behind bars.

2. Describe what you look like.

Not exactly, but almost, tall, dark, and handsome. Let's call it slightly tall, dark, and furry.

What do you like about how you look?

People love my curls and they are me. My smile is genuine and infectious. Supposedly my legs and booty are nicely shaped. My 'brow'-fros have been awesome lately. The sexiest woman I've ever known thinks I'm gorgeous, so even though I'm not sure why, I guess I like myself exactly as I am for the first time.

Is there something you wish you could change?

My forehead appears to be slowly becoming a five-head. It sure would be nice to not have that patch of butt fur trying to escape my shorts up my back.

3. Do you have a family? If so, tell me about them.

My family is the roots, the trunk, the leaves that I need to still bloom. They are the foundation that keeps me standing tall in this swamp. They turn the sun into energy in this darkness and keep me breathing in this miasma.

My family is huge, too, and not just by blood. Family is an earned privilege and it cannot be broken once established. There is no greater loyalty than giving time and love to someone falsely (or otherwise) imprisoned. My family consists, first and foremost, of my beautiful, brilliant, wise, brave partner, Gin, and my kind, strong, smart, athletic son, Dmitrius Karma. It also includes my amazing parents, nine siblings (especially Marigot), and a couple dozen confidants (special love to Nancee, Sam, Trish, Seth, Jack, Joan, and Jason).

4. Do you have children? If so, what do you most love about them? What do you miss about them?

I have the most amazing son in the entire world, Dmitrius Karma. I am also honored to be the future father of Veda, who will undoubtedly be wise and delightful. That is a great thrill daily. Dmitrius shines my pride right now, showing the world that he is a young man of incredible character, staying close as he grows. He has been my best buddy since the day he was born, and his well being is my biggest concern from this situation. Yet he has made it through with incredible resilience, thriving in every way. He's bright and doing well in school and an absolute superstar in multiple sports. What I love most about him, though, is his heart. He is full of nothing but kindness for the world and is a warrior for decency and diversity even at 12. What I miss most about him are the carefree times we had together: nature explorations and hikes, imagination games, endless squirt gun fights from the cache that lived permanently in our trunk, and laughing while up too late.

5. What are your goals?

*To be the best partner possible for Gin, bringing her joy and support every single day, matching how she loves me so well.
*To be a father that makes a positive difference, bestowing health, inspiration, principles, and happiness daily.
*To give more to the world than I take from it.
*To teach and inspire every day.
*To elevate those around me wherever I am.
*To spread kindness, respect, and tolerance.
*To educate others about the importance of the social world and bonds.

6. If you could leave prison for a day, what would you do?

I would spend the entire day in the warm embrace and smile of Gin, my incredible, loving goddess of a partner.

There would have to be a feast of great company and food with Dmitrius and my closest family, too…but if I only had one day, I would have to spend it making love and laughter, most likely never getting fully dressed.

7. Do you believe your life has a purpose or mission? What is it?

My purpose has been clarified during this prison experience. It starts by being the best partner, father, and friend I can be, as I have the most impact on the lives closest to me. More broadly, my life's purpose is to love and spread the message and power of love, while being a voice for the voiceless, promoting diversity, tolerance, and respect for all.

8. What do you think makes a good friend?

The recipe for gourmet friendship includes trust, loyalty, unconditional support, laughter, and adventure. With a good friend, we not only can but are eager to get in a car for days of road trippin', even unaware of our destination, but knowing that the journey and every pit stop will make precious memories.

9. What's your biggest life lesson so far?

Treat people, yourself, nature, and the universe how you would be treated and how you want the world to be. Turns out that people and the world have an incredible tendency to meet expectations. What we expect is what we get because our thoughts have such power, and this is especially true of social interactions. Hence, optimism, kindness, and respect are the keys to a happy life. This has, notably, proven even more true in prison, where my adamant respect for others has been returned in kind.

10. What advice would you give to your younger self or a child in a similar position as you were when you were young?

*Unabashedly pursue your passions without regard for finance or prestige.
*It's all about the people! Put them above dollars, things, or convenience, always.
*Believe in yourself in everything you do. Stop worrying about what others think.
*Proudly use your big brain, but not exclusively. Balance it with heart, of which there is never too much.

11. What does it feel like to live in prison?

Like being invisible and voiceless, alone even as I live in sardine proximity. We are deliberately, fully institutionalized, robbed of our names, identities, and ability to touch the world. Everything that makes us human—affection, social bonds, communication—is taken away. It feels dehumanizing. Everyone outside suspects that the violence is the worst, but it's actually the isolation from loved ones.

12. How do you feel about the prison system or the justice system?

I *feel* like boiling rage and frustration in a cave of inky black depression because of how it has unfairly hurt my son, my partner, my parents, and myself. So, instead, I tend to *think* and *know* about it intellectually to stay positive, productive, and sane. I *know* that the US system is not only a failure, but it is entirely counterproductive and contrary to its professed philosophical origins of helping make society safer and helping people be more productive citizens. It is punitive and vindictive, and that never helps anyone. It has no conscience, consuming souls and hope gluttonously with lengthy sentences that lack support or resources. It provides a stigmatized social life sentence of degradation that belies the myth of second chances in this land. It may not be the worst system in the world, but it is by far the most repressive and ineffective of any nation claiming freedom. It is expensive and cruel, costing families and individuals so much that all of society pays.

13. What makes you laugh?

Nothing makes me laugh better or harder than hearing a deep belly laugh from Gin or Dmitrius. Laughter is contagious, spread by love. If it's just me otherwise, I am an enigma in the placement of my funny bone—it moves all over the place! My favorite sitcom is Modern Family, though I lack the patience for nearly all others. I love satire of the illogic of conservatism and consumerism so wonderfully delivered by the likes of Colbert, Sam Bee, John Oliver, and the almighty Jon Stewart (RIP, original Daily Show!). But I am also amused by farts, humping, Chris Farley, and other fundamentally adolescent baselines. Nothing, though, is funnier than live improv, the greatest acting and comedy around.

14. Finish the sentence:
If I could change the world, I would start at home, how I live, which means being there every day.

*...have all societies remain unique but organize and function with unity, common good, and sustainability as priorities, not consumption and commodification.
*...eliminate profit from health, death, and imprisonment. Ugly, garish, obscene that it ever happens.
*...undo all that has been done in the name of the expansionist, greedy insecurities of white men's (I am one physically, but not spiritually) cultures and weapons in the history of the world.

I believe that Dmitrius, Gin, and I are changing the world for better.
*...that all things are connected and energy lasts forever, so positive energy is both a gift and a purpose.
*...in Karma.
*...love is stronger than anything else in the universe, even hatred, so the only way to defeat hate and fear is with love and kindness.
*...talent and character are equally distributed across the population, but (sadly) opportunity is not.

I wish I could spend every day in Gin's arms and Dmitrius's company, living on laughter and shared adventure, paying the bills by trading in the joy we spread.
*...I had found this heightened love and patience without having to go through this mess so that no one I love had to hurt with me.
*...everyone was committed to putting the earth and others ahead of themselves at least once each day.
*...I never had to hear another white male complain about being discriminated against ever again. Boo-fucking-hoo, you have to work as hard as everyone else for once!

I am inspired by love.
*…Gin and Dmitrius.
*…nature, in its power and its splendor.
*…helping people.
*…fighting oppression.
*…the divine feminine strength.
*…diversity.
*…roses that grow in concrete.

15. Please share anything else you'd like. This is your space. And your voice.

Two poems. I fancy myself a poet and often believe that I can express much more depth much more eloquently in many fewer words this way. The first one of these is an optimist's love poem considering how, despite living my worst nightmare, I was able to find the greatest love I could ever imagine. I have found that maintaining character and purpose here, staying human, requires the ability to see the beauty even in the dark. I am in the best relationship I've ever imagined finding and it was ignited and shines brighter every day because we both do so. In a nightmare we found a love to define always.

"Only Here"

It is only in the darkness
that we rely on
all our senses
and deepest instincts
so only here could I
fully feel your love

It is only in confinement
where freedom's edges

can be sharpened
so only here could I
whet and hone
my always appetite
It is only in the winter
that we dream
to survive the cold
and hunger
so only here could I
rest and see the world
of hope beyond reason

It is only in the unknown
that we ask
questions that seek
new galaxies' awareness
so only here could I
learn to see the moon goddess
reflected in midnight seas

It was only in these surface miseries
where I found my inner compass
inspired by love to love
and love first...always
I thank the devils and demons fire
distilling me to my essence
how I stumbled my way here to...
...always

This second piece is a more esoteric musing, examining
western culture's current need to extract and commodify
all things in the natural world. I read an article about
private companies bidding to mine the moon and
meteors. Is nothing sacred anymore?! This one was

selected also because it garnered the approval of my poetic mentor and idol, the wise and charismatic Nikki Giovanni. Everyone who seeks truth and insight should spend a night reading her.

"Cosmic Priorities"

if they mine
the moon
for platinum
where will the dreams
find lustre?
or will they all dull?

if they drill
asteroids
for water
where will goddesses
find tears
to shed
when the rivers
run dry?

why must men make priority
of extraction,
a commodity
of the cosmos?

can't wonder be
incentive enough,
infinity's possibility
ours without
ownership?

Taj and I have written many letters back and forth, and continue to do so. Gin and I share emails, as well.

In fact, the way he has shared with me about his relationship with Gin—his Queen with a capital "Q" as he calls her—has touched me and inspired me. The way he has written about his masculinity— "blasting mountaintops for profit, / diverting rivers, mounting trophy heads / impress not my masculinity / like planting trees and growing peace"—has spoken to my soul and to our collective experience.

But much of our writing is personal, always bordering on (or, rather, falling into!) the nerdy. We discuss poetry and meditate on books. I have told him about men in my life and he has offered advice. We have talked about elections, the UN Human Rights Council, and Alice Walker. So I do not believe most of it belongs here.

Instead, I have shared a few moments that have shed light on his role in this project (he has connected me with several men whose voices are published in this book and several who are not) and the topic, I suppose, we came to talk about: prison. And, lastly, one of those sparkling moments, a connector, when I got to meet his lovely Gin in person when she was visiting New York.

All of that is below. But, before I leave you with it, one note from Taj himself, from a June 7th letter to me as he typed it on the only device offered by the Virginia Department of Corrections, at a price to those who can afford it, for email:

"please forgive the lack of capitalization," he wrote. "typing on this tiny device they give us (circa 2006 technology) does not auto cap sentence beginnings and manually doing so is tedious. So, shorthand, in just that sense. please bear with me. :) "

June 20, 2018

Taj,

On Sunday (Father's Day), you kept coming to mind. I think I had taken for granted that Father's Day is a day of celebration, forgetting that it also is a day that may carry pain. And, by that, I'm thinking about the men in prison without their children, and the children of fathers in prison without their dads (and, now, horrifically, the immigrant children torn from their parents at our borders)—and this list is far from comprehensive. So, tell me, what was your Father's Day like and did you get to speak to Dmitrius? Were fathers able to receive visitors that day and what was the tone in your prison that day? I also never got to tell you that I love the way you described Dmitrius to me in your "Share Your Voice" responses: you described him as "bright," full of "heart" and "nothing but kindness," and a "warrior for decency." The way you see him with love and clarity and how you see him in his power will only fuel his growth. It's empowering to know the men who raise us believe in us.

I'm thrilled to meet with your radiant Gin soon, too. I promise to bring her that smile you asked for. It's the least I can do.

In perpetual thanks,
Ashley

June 22, 2018

Ashley,

quite the question you asked about father's day. did you really manage to rethink father's day here on your own? my own family doesn't even fully grasp it. I'm not generally maudlin, either, but that day and Dmitrius's birthday are the two worst days here. they are days we devoted always to together time and adventures, something we always did best. I don't think of it as a day for celebrating me, but rather one for our bond. it was also my dad's birthday the same day this year.

thank you for sending good energy. this year was better than most. my mom came all the way from new mexico and visited both days of the weekend. typically we only get either even or odd days—visits are only weekends, for a few hours, but I got special approval since she came so far. on Saturday, she surprised me bringing a brother I've not seen in over a year. on Sunday, gin joined her and that was a beautiful togetherness. and Dmitrius has often had tough times that day, too, missing me. this year, though, he led his team to the flag football championship as the quarterback that day, playing well but also being a vocal leader. so he was stoked, and that helped.

more broadly, the tenor here that day is generally subdued. nearly all men here are fathers, almost all deeply caring ones.

I also have an essay I'm writing the next couple weeks about visitation dis-encouragement by DOC. suffice it to say that they know it's helpful and claim they promote it, but the opposite is true. gin is amazing about it, but they generally go out of their way to make it uncomfortable and shaming for everyone involved. I'm hoping to get the essay in the Marshall Project, I think. just found out about them.

in solidarity,
taj

p.s. have fun with gin. I'm so excited you two are meeting up!

June 27, 2018

Taj,

This is just a quick note to say it was such a joy to meet your lovely Gin today. She is kind and thoughtful, talented, and made me laugh!

I teased her that one of my favorite things about her is that when we arrived at the restaurant and realized they only had plastic utensils, she had us take a trip back to her car so she could pull out not one but two reusable forks made by a friend from Hawaii. (She gifted me the second one!) I usually carry my own set of reusable utensils, but had forgotten mine at home. She is a woman after my own heart, with an added touch of generosity!

We talked about prison, of course, and about you, but also about lomi lomi, yoga, horseback riding therapy, her pets Dusty and Cilantro (I'm now following their Instagram page), plastic pollution, and her experience at Prospect Park this weekend.

I feel lucky to have both of you in my life and am glad I got to share her today.

Thinking happy thoughts of you today, too.

And, finally, the last thing: Gin told me you were in solitary confinement for a year. I'm sure one email cannot explain it but, if you had to begin, what would you tell me about it?

Warmly,
Ashley

P.S. Thank you for continuing to share this project. What I'm doing wouldn't be possible without you.

July 7, 2018

Hello, my friend!

we just got done with a week of lockdown. one of the worst aspects of this place, particularly for leaving us out of touch.

glad you enjoyed gin. I got to see a really great photo of you two. big smiles. human connections are so wonderful, particularly so serendipitous.

just a quick note here back for now. working on getting caught up.

thank you for the positive feedback on this project, but unnecessary. it's your baby. all I'm doing is getting the chance to look good for spreading word on such a great thing run by such a true, deep person. same goal as my own work, and you put in all the effort and have all the charisma that leaves everyone here thanking me. sweet deal for me :)

you asked about my year of desperate misery in solitary. I will share entirely soon. it was the most traumatic, debilitating thing about this experience. it crushed my extrovert soul. it broke me. it's a big, long story, though. are you sure you want to go down that rabbit hole? besides losing the time with Dmitrius, that was the worst part of this. it will be an ugly account and may take a minute to compile.

I have never written about it, probably for that reason. it reflects my weakness and depression. but many loved ones tell me I should because it is an extreme case on a contemporary issue.

anyway, I'll write more soon and respond more soon to other stuff. just wanted to get back.

cheers and solidarity,
taj

August 14, 2018

Ashley,

Here you go, my friend...

To someone who has never been in "the hole," "solitary," or officially the Segregated Housing Unit, it cannot be readily described or understood. even to others who have served time behind bars, I believe it is difficult to describe. it was like being alive physically, but slowly watching myself fade away from life beyond my shell, like the photo of Michael J. Fox in *Back to the Future*. yet, in this version, I was stuck in a concrete and steel box where the lights never go off and I couldn't do anything to stop my emotional, social, spiritual decay.

on top of that, it was like drowning while I could see the light of day above water's edge. it was like being invisible, voiceless, helpless, no matter how strong my body and my mind has always been. I could reach out for the life preserver but never quite grasp it. every breath a struggle, never full day light but never the full release of death.

yes, I became near suicidal while in solitary. all that time alone with nothing but the reality of my incapacity drove me to despair. I thought about it often, I must but hate to admit, even wished death would just happen from wishing. imagine having worked all your adult life to build a career, a family, a reputation for social activism and kindness, then to have it all suddenly, unexpectedly, disappear overnight. now, I'm in this box where the lights above never go off and there's no one to talk with about it. a call or two a day, maybe, twenty five bucks a pop, all my savings gone in a couple months. some letters trickle in. everyone I love is trying to help, but they can do so little, too. imagine, no physical human contact or affection at all for months. I knew I shouldn't be in that situation, hadn't earned the accusations or the pain...but how could I stay strong as the loneliness and loss kept compounding? I'd already had life vanish instantly, yet now the process of trial preparation and media provocation dragged out that vanishing slowly, repeating the pain, threatening to keep it ongoing for the rest of my life for something I didn't do. after 10 months of being alone in my worst nightmare, stolen from my son and the rest of my family, a feminist pacifist not permitted to even walk to the shower without shackles, they told me that if I did not falsely cop a plea and accept many years, I'd never see daylight again. what would you do? some people say that they would never plead guilty when innocent on principle. well, my principle was seeing my son again and I'd seen the justice system fail. hell, I taught all about it before this. and then I was tortured by silence and loneliness, an extrovert unable to socialize, a father with a son too young to understand and too loved to risk losing forever.

the fact that so many of the emotionally toughest men in society here spend so much time proclaiming, unasked, about how they don't care about going to seg demonstrates how miserable it is in reality. such posturing is reserved for fending off our biggest fears. this is why the hole is often used not for safety but for psychological control reasons. I went there not because I was a danger to anyone. no one had ever accused me of violence and I'd threatened none. the prosecutor and the jail wanted to win an improvised case against me lacking evidence, them my only accusers. I lived in a hole for nearly a year before they finally broke my will with an impossible choice. I caved. the darkness of eternal fluorescent light echoing off otherwise silent concrete walls made sleeping on a steel cot too difficult even for the depressed. instead, I lay there and listened to the doubts and uncertainty of solitude tear down my will. humane treatment requires direct human interaction and the opportunity for social support. our social bonds are the very trait that allowed us to evolve such big, rational brains. death is preferable to unbounded isolation after a certain point, or so it seemed to me at the time.

all these words, and all I can say to anyone who doubts the terror of extended solitary is, try going even one week without a single smile, hug, or conversation, even without the accusations and threats.

taj

George

Three.

May 25, 2018

Hi Ashley!

Please call me George, as not many do. Hearing George allows me to be more responsible for who I have become.

1. Introduce yourself! Tell me a little about you.

I am 39 years of age, and I have been incarcerated since before my nineteenth birthday, and I'm surprisingly not bitter at the fact.

Although I had entered prison with no more than a seventh grade education, I've survived it by first taking my worst and making it into everything I needed it to be. I recreated myself by discovering empathy, and applying it towards our justice system and its representatives in order to be freed from its normally unbearable circumstances. Despite having never set foot in a legal library prior to 2011, I had managed to win and have reversed three times, decisions in my case.

I do attempt to be as Christian as possible on a daily basis. But most importantly, I am in love with my spirituality, and I enjoy hard work. The worst pain ever endured was not having the correct person to have noticed that I had become more…

2. Describe what you look like. What do you like about how you look? Is there something you wish you could change?

It's always somehow difficult for me to describe my appearance. Where the best of me has gone unnoticed by me for so long. It hurts having to look at something that everyone refuses to see. I do however have all of my teeth (lol) and I am very physically fit at six foot and 216 pounds.

I do love how my smile always makes me feel better even during those impossible times. "More people should see George." (lol)!!

3. Do you have family? If so, tell me about them.

Two sisters one whom is biracial, four nephews, no brothers; a step father whom I've had the unique pleasure of admiring for most of my life for loving my mom even at times I thought her to be unlovable, and him deserving of more.

4. Do you have children? If so, what do you most love about them? What do you miss about them?

One daughter, whom I share a fantastic relationship with. Despite her present Job as a jailer, and her stubbornness: I love the fact that she is able to be strong for us both even when she is not. Oddly enough I never miss her; She is so much a part of me that I have never had to feel her absence.

5. What are your goals?

Oh, to someday invent a tool that allows people to instantly see more of who someone is and less of who they are perceived to be. (MUCH LIKE YOU ASHLEY)

6. If you could leave prison for a day, what would you do?

Visit the San Diego coastline for one hour.

7. Do you believe your life has a purpose or specific mission? What is it?

To endure, so that others may become what they were intended to be.

8. What do you think makes a good friend?

Someone who shares a love for you that's neither dependent on what you will or won't do; Nor on what you can or can't do. Someone who loves you even when it is less convenient for them. Yes, now that's a friend! (It should be much like a relationship you share with God.)

9. What's your biggest life lesson so far?

It's the love that you feel for others that makes you who you are able to become in this world. Accept its responsibilities.

10. What advice would you give to your younger self or to a child in a similar position as you were when you were young?

Discover 'YOUR REASONS WHY' defining who you are.

11. What does it feel like to live in prison?

Unlovable.

12. How do you feel about the prison system or the justice system?

That 'it' has failed its responsibilities, and even worse lacks an identity for its existence.

13. What makes you laugh?

Hearing the laughter of others. I often times feel as if they are laughing especially for me.

14. Finish the sentence:
I believe whenever you are given opportunities at either love or life, Be sure to live them both.

Thank You Ashley!! Yes you do have my expressed permission to publish my words if found fitting, and as deemed necessary.

GEORGE J. GREEN

June 4, 2018

George,

Thank you for taking the time and the attention to answer my Share Your Voice questions. It's an honor to know you are willing to open yourself to me and let me hear you. Listening is my privilege.

In fact, you wrote a lot in your letter about feeling unseen and the pain that comes with not being recognized for who you truly are. It hurts my heart to hear that you've felt disappeared at times, that you've felt like "something that everyone refuses to see," and that living in prison feels "unlovable."

I wish I alone could heal that in you but, of course, I alone do not have those powers. What I can do is offer you my friendship and the awareness that we are connected, most certainly more alike than different. I want to see all of you.

In fact, I am certain you are not alone. Before I read your letter, I had been meditating all week on the idea of feeling seen. And, as I was running through my neighborhood one morning, I realized that I am holding on to anger over not feeling seen and recognized for who I am.

So when I opened your email and read it through, I felt a kinship: "Ah, yes," I thought, someone else patiently waiting to break free: not only out of prison, but into your fullness. Someone else seeking recognition for everything they carry in their heart and in their soul.

Of course, my journey is not yours and I do not wish to write mine over yours. All I wish to do is thank you for sharing and for helping me feel seen and heard simply by you having the courage and strength and vulnerability to tell me your feelings.

I also want you to know that I believe in you. That I hear your intelligence in your words but, more than that, I feel your passion. Your heart is compassionate and bold. You are sensitive, my favorite type. And, by this, I do not mean weak, I mean someone in tune enough with himself and the universe to feel and to hear. You have vision that meets action: you have transformed yourself, bursting open the cocoon.

In closing, know that you are loved and worthy of being loved.

At the bottom of this email, I've included one last thing: a short poem from my latest book about becoming. I have a feeling you will recognize its spirit.

In friendship,
Ashley

There is nothing
I want to scream more than
"I am bursting!"
And then
I think of a seedling
crashing through its own walls,
pushing up against soil—
lifting the whole world above it
to open,
and I think,
"Yes, of course."
Did I think birth
was free from pain?

—you can do it

June 4, 2018

One of the greatest days of my time came when a single message exacted purpose; A BRILLIANT Friend (you) wrote reminding me of my self worth. Giving emphasis to a blinding fact that I had been genuinely afraid of becoming who or what I was meant to be. You impacted my most intimate feelings by saying how I had been truly loved, and that I had been forever worthy of such a blessing.

Today I was BETTER. A better father, son, listener, friend. Someone who has been created to exist, and not just to live. I felt your spirit carrying me. Holding and protecting me as a mother would her child.

Ashley, YOU are beautiful, my friend. Absolutely gorgeous! More of you will certainly dictate a better me for the future. Oh, that reminds me. When I spoke to Taj about how beautiful you are, he asked if I had received a picture of you (smile). I didn't want to tell him that all that I was feeling was a result of your first email, so I simply said, "Her words stand miles over any physical attributes."

You are who you are especially for me. You are great so that I am better. You alone was able to take away the hurt and pain, although momentarily.

Thank you for all that you are becoming Asti. And as my friend, I love you.

Lastly, tell me what are some things you most admire about yourself?

What do you expect from a friend and what does having a friend feel like for you?

What's something that's most important in your life?

What makes you upset or annoyed?

What are some of your favorite foods?

What is it about you that you believe makes you beautiful to me?

How often do you do yoga and, no, I'm not doing yoga! What would my guys think?

Your comprehensive skills are unique, special. Would you consider it a "gift"?

Are you willing to allow me to see all of YOU? AND NOT JUST THROUGH BEAUTIFUL POETRY. (By the way, you made me cry happy tears for the first time ever!)

Ashley i again feel, and it is wonderful!! You have true gumption. Further your spirit has character and unmatched grit. Poor old George, you completely did away with him!

In absolutely appreciation of YOU,
George

June 5, 2018

I LIKE YOU. I HAD THE BEST DAY. ALL BECAUSE
YOU MADE ME BETTER. THANK YOU!! GEORGE

June 6, 2018

George,

Your emails made me happy, too.

What I can assure you is that you were created with purpose and you live this, in part, by expressing yourself —sharing you. It takes a strong man to be vulnerable and honest. We rarely say what we mean but you have not hidden behind artifice. In your email, you have expressed exactly what you feel. That is both bold and inspiring: it has encouraged me to be honest with you and in my life. Any other way is stifling.

That's one of the things I love about writing letters: in them, we often express what we may not say aloud.

I think what I am most blessed by is that you called me a mother: "holding and protecting me as a mother would her child," you wrote. I never felt a calling to have children of my own, but I do feel a call to mother—to nourish, to support, to protect, to defend, to honor, to see, to grow. Thank you for reminding me that mothers don't need to have physical children.

Let me answer your questions:

1. What do I admire most about myself?
I appreciate you asking me this question because, ordinarily, I would not answer it aloud (publicly). I would plead modesty! Instead, today, I will claim it. I admire my gentleness and compassion when, for so long, I didn't know that I was. I admire all the people who have made me and the life that has made me who I am. I admire my

passion and my furious belief in my own purpose. I will not rest until I have lived it.

2. What do I expect from a friend and what does having a friend feel like for me?
Great question. I expect a friend to stimulate my mind and my soul. I expect kindness from both of us. I expect punctuality (lol) and someone who feels an intense call to live their purpose. The very few true friends I have had have felt like tremendous laughter and like, when I see them, I light up.

3. What's something that's most important in my life?
Not something but someone: my mom. We learn from each other and grow together and she listens tirelessly to me. I am very lucky.

4. What makes me upset or annoyed?
I'm sure my family can answer that question better than I can. ;)

5. What are some of my favorite foods?
Avocados, for sure. I've been making this awesome smoothie lately: avocado, cucumber, spinach, and mint leaves.
What I love (but don't eat) are Cheerios.

6. What is it about me that I believe makes me beautiful to you?
Instead, let me tell you what I think is beautiful about you: your openness, your willingness to take an interest in others, the way I imagine you treat others with respect because Taj spoke so beautifully of you and I respect him greatly, and your commitment to your own transformation.

7. How often do I do yoga?
Almost every day! And there's nothing to be embarrassed about. Real men do yoga. You can tell your guys I said so. ;)

8. Would I consider my set of skills a gift?
I'm honored that you even asked. I am blessed to be myself and want to be nothing other than me. I hope everyone else may discover this about themselves, too: they are exactly as they are meant to be.

You told me that my words have made you feel happy for the first time in a long time. Thank you, but I am simply seeing your light and reflecting it back to you. You've got everything within.

With gratitude,
Ashley

P.S. Tell me what it's like to be a father. I want to know what it's like to create new life and watch it grow.

June 6, 2018

Cheerios, Ashley!! (I am smiling my butt off.)

Yes, I hope to be able to learn a lot from Taj. I especially appreciate him for making things better for me.

You speak loosely about energy and wisdom. I want to know EVERYTHING. (Asti, come clean!) What things have you experienced…Teach me!

Ashley, by age 13, I had been sexually molested by two separate female relatives, repeatedly, because of my, let's say, "maturity" at an early age. Kendra, my daughter, and one of the greatest treasures of this world had been forced to also suffer a similar fate, albeit not by family. But mainly due to my mistakes, my absence, and therefore my inability to protect her. I failed her, beyond any doubt. So you see, Ashley, it's by her character alone that I can consider myself a father.

If only I had been stronger to resist, I would be better for her. My attempt at loving her through my pain wasn't enough. So it has been her who raised a once needing boy into a father. In her strength, she had to become my nurturer in order for our relationship to have been made as it is. I had not been courageous for her, Ashley. Where proper schooling, any sense of responsibility, and valued expectations would have made the difference for her, I failed my baby. Never should any parent take this for granted. Sorry.

Tell me more about your mom. She seems great. I admired instantly how she made you feel. Boy, would i love to know her favorite perfume! (Oh, my mom has become one of my biggest fans, and we share a great relationship. My dad, not so much. But I don't hate him.)

Enough about me. Your passion is intoxicating, Asti. I would love for you to see all of me.

Ashley, my birthday is August 19, and I'm thinking of maybe using that day to walk away from (a lot)…starting my life over. I am truly a great person, therefore I need to give me a real chance at becoming more. Kendra deserves it also.

One last thing—I've decided to send you a picture of me, understanding that your imagination shouldn't be wasted on my appearance. You have books to write. ;)

Thanking you,
George

June 7, 2018

Good morning, beautiful! Allow today to be for you exciting and tantalizing. Meet people. Allow them the pleasure of knowing who you are. Be exotic and purposeful.

I've decided against sending you a picture of me just yet.

Truly,
George

June 10, 2018

George,

I thank you for your patience with my reply. Know that I have been working a lot (and answering lots of letters!), so I may be a few days delayed in my response, but I read everything you wrote when you wrote it and took it in.

I also want to thank you for what you wrote in your last short email: "Meet people. Allow them the pleasure of knowing who you are." That is both beautiful and sagacious and I appreciate you for reminding me to share all of me with the world. We could all use that reminder.

I'm also thinking about what you said about the violence you survived as a child. I just want you to know, "maturity" or not, you did not deserve that. In fact, "maturity" has nothing to do with it at all: the shape of your body or your being has no responsibility for what happened: do not take that blame upon yourself or justify it. There is no "strong enough to resist" sexual violence at 13—or ever.

And may Kendra's ability to forgive and nourish be a testament, a guiding light, for others. Only in forgiving ourselves and others can we carry less pain.

As for my passion—yes, I am passionate and I hope it is intoxicating because it is not mine alone; it stems from existence, a collective soul.

In that vein, I wanted to tell you what I saw of you in your last letter: yes, I felt some pain and some desire but, also, I saw your humor. You made me laugh when you called me by my last name and said, "ASTI, come clean!" In fact, in that moment I felt like you saw me because you knew I've got something else going on beneath the surface—like you felt the energy hidden between my words. "What things have you experienced," you wrote.

And I laughed also when you said, "I've decided to send you a picture of me. Understanding that your imagination shouldn't be wasted on my appearance…You have books to write." Witty and suave in that you captured my brainy sense of humor.

This is all to say I'm glad to know you're enjoying our exchange. I am, too. I cannot be the source of your transformation, your starting over, but I can support you in it. Only you can rise like the phoenix from the ashes and renew yourself. As your friend, I hope you find continual renewal in your life and in yourself. May the power to refresh yourself spring always from your heart!

I know I didn't answer all of your questions (about my mom, for one). I will. And I want to know about your relationship with your mom, too. I felt what I wrote above is enough for now.

Sincerely,
Ashley

June 11, 2018

You are beautiful. Too busy, but beautiful yet and still.

I agree with you whole heartedly. I am my reasons why.

Ashley, your obligation to your work and the others that you communicate with and help is important to me also. I do not wish to interfere; I will slow down on my emails to make things easier for you. Just know that I dig the way your heart beats. I like the way that you express yourself through your words. It is, to me, a very unique quality. I will forever be appreciative of how I am able to feel because of who you are.

In Truth, your old friend,
George

June 15, 2018

George,

...It's funny because, for the past few minutes, I've been sitting here at my computer in the silence of type-less-ness, as I, unusually, don't know what to say next. And as I'm sitting here doing, it seems, nothing, I've noticed my desk and all that sits on it around me and I realized it probably tells a lot about me. So let me share it with you:

The desk I use is an old, antique-looking desk from my great aunt who passed away a few years ago. I cherish it because it was hers. To the left of me on my desk is a postal scale which sits atop two issues of the *New Yorker*. Two issues because I never seem to be able to catch up with the magazines as they come, though they are so delicious every time I open them and dive in to read. The postal scale because, earlier this morning, I was weighing packages of organic skincare products that I make and shipping them off to customers.

Above that sits a few things: a card whose cover is sunflowers. It's from one of my friends, Britney, who is incarcerated in Texas and within it is a psalm. It reminds me of her, so it makes me smile and I've kept it on my desk for a month now. In the left corner there are several organic essential oils for diffusing peace throughout my room, and leaning up against the wall behind the oils is a drawing my friend Alicia, who's also living in a Texas prison right now, made for me.

On the right side of my desk are lots of papers: emails printed out from you and Taj, and letters in envelopes from other friends in prisons across the country. I also have a stack of stamps that say "Love" on them for mailing my replies.

There are papers of vegan recipes (most notably, avocado pancakes, zucchini noodle salad, and what's called an "avocado beauty smoothie"). There's a standing container for all my pens and pencils, markers, scissors, and even a ruler (the ruler I rarely use); a skincare product of my own creation, a lamp that oddly doesn't work, and, lastly, a photo of me and my friend Brittany. Brittany is the founder of a nonprofit that supports families of new babies with Down syndrome across the country and I serve on the Board of Directors of the organization. Brittany is sassy, fun, courageous, a great self-advocate and an even better friend, and she happens to have Down syndrome.

Oh, and I paused typing to take a sip of water. There is always a big mason jar of water with a reusable glass straw (plastic straws get thrown away and pollute our oceans and the creatures living in our oceans, so I avoid them) sitting on my desk when I'm working.

So, tell me, what are the possessions you keep with you? Or tell me anything—I want to know what's on your mind and in your heart.

Sincerely,
Ashley

June 16, 2018

Ashley,

Okay, let's go, my possessions:

In front of me is a list of nine exercises which I do for 45 seconds each daily. Then there is a statement I've written that reminds me to become more. On the side of my bed I have a prayer book for men. I have some legal books, a book which helps me with social skills, *50 Shades Darker*, which happens to be my favorite book—only because of the complexity for which he loved her. She meant even more than his greatest desires.

On my locker I have Healing Damaged Emotions prayer cards, a separate set of prayer cards for wisdom, a parent's prayer, and one for justice.

There are two different types of soap (Dove for my face, Dial for my body); Lady's Speed Stick (it smells the best); coconut oil for my scalp; razors; powder; toothpaste; toothbrush; mouthwash; Vo5 shampoo (no hair, so that's funny!); beard trimmers; Suave lotion; multivitamins; cotton swabs; prayer oil; and a TV that I barely watch.

What surrounds me are circumstances that I can't control —a broken man that will give anything to be able to live again, to smile just because, to love someone in ways that are unimaginable.

I love because I hope I'm more than broken promises. I love because I am still yet a boy who wants desperately to remove himself from the pain. I love because my mind, body, and soul has been commanded to do so by my God.

No games. I thank you more often than anyone I know. I enjoy your emails more than any other things in my life. Although surrounded by the worst circumstances imaginable, I find absolute comfort in you.

Oh, I hope you laughed out loud for me today.

George

June 19, 2018

Ashley,

Hey, I am sure that you are just as busy as ever. Just know that I am cheering for you, praying for your happiness, and enjoying your strength.

George

July 7, 2018

Ashley I am now crying as it is vastly becoming apparent that more of me remains under circumstances much too much to bare. My imprisonment overpowers my will to live. It hurts.

Although my heart is noble...uncontrollably, lonesomeness invades my mind.

I picture clearly one day becoming perfected, miles away from sadness. But for now, I am trapped in a world that's not my own; uncompromising what should I do? How do I live through this?

I envision dancing under the stars, as we laugh and play. Freed from the burdens of having time that's owed.

Never easy, I continue to see me. Full of hope, and true grit. I'm forced to reconcile with a spirit that knows its difference.

It's now 7:42am, and 'Spiritual Bliss' as I have come accustomed to knowing it, has settled my misery. A once tormented mind has compelled itself, no longer fueled by bitterness. I see more.

George

Lisa

Four.

June 11, 2018

Lisa,

I read your poem, "You Can't Bully Me!" in the California Coalition for Women Prisoner's *Fire Inside* Spring addition and I had to reach out. I love your courage in the poem and your integrity. You have learned one of the most powerful lessons for all of us to learn: who we are is not defined by anyone else. Thank you for expressing yourself fully.

My favorite line was this: "You helped me to be the most wonderful, kind, respectful woman that I need to be." I like this line for its clarity: you know that kindness and respect are what make a woman (or any person) great.

I'm an author who is currently working on a book project that will feature the voices of those who are incarcerated because I believe we are far more alike than different, and this deserves to be highlighted. After hearing your powerful voice, I wanted to extend an invitation to you to participate. I would be honored if you chose to spread your voice through this project.

The instructions are on the following page. Feel free to reach out to me with any questions about me or the project.

With gratitude and respect,
Ashley

June 23, 2018

1. Introduce yourself! Tell me a little about you:

I am a very honest person before anything else. I learn each day about myself. In prison, I have to teach *everyone* how to treat me because I am transgender.

I am very passionate about my life as who I am, "Lisa." I give everything I have to make it a better place for my trans sisters and the LGBT population. I love life and I see the world as colorful, not black and white.

I love to watch all sports, but wouldn't play because I am truly a girly girl.

I am an author. I have been published almost 60 times. I am also a feminist. I believe the only difference between men and women is their gender orientation. But even with saying that, I am not defined by my gender. I am still female because it is who I see, not what others think.

2. Describe what you look like. What do you like about how you look? Is there something you wish you could change?

I am 5'9", long strawberry blonde hair, and blue eyes. I like everything about me. I would not change a thing. If I were to leave this earth today, I would be content with knowing and loving myself as I am.

3. Do you have family? If so, tell me about them.

My mom committed suicide when I was 17. She was so beautiful, but she couldn't handle an abusive marriage to an alcoholic man. To this day, I've not forgotten her scent and how much I love her.

My father is still alive. I have no contact. He was not very much a part of my life. He and my mother divorced when I was five.

I have a sister that I don't hear much from. I don't spend my time trying to figure out why. She is my sister and I love her. The family I am close to are my mom's sister and one of her daughters. We have kept in touch over the 24 years I have been in prison. They keep me going by just being there for me and accepting me for who I am.

4. Do you have children? If so, what do you most love about them? What do you miss about them?

No children.

5. What are your goals?

My goal is to get out and advocate for those who have been silenced because of bullies, gender, or race. And to go to schools and show kids that you can be who you say you are.

6. If you could leave prison for a day, what would you do?

What a question. I would get on a plane and go see my family in Ohio.

7. Do you believe your life has a purpose or specific mission? What is it?

My life now is driven by purpose. It is to speak up and stand out to make a difference in others' lives.

8. What do you think makes a good friend?

A good friend is someone who is honest, even when you don't want to hear it.

9. What's your biggest life lesson so far?

My biggest life lesson is that it has taken me three times in prison for me to see that I am a good person and that I do care about others.

10. What advice would you give to your younger self or to a child in a similar position as you were when you were young?

This is a difficult question, but I think I wish that I would have known that people truly loved me. So I would make sure that children would know they are loved.

11. What does it feel like to live in prison?

Every day is a struggle. Even 24 years later. Even more difficult as a transgender because people are fake, play head games, and I always have to be on guard from everyone. And others do not like a smart girl. Everything I do is pretty much controlled by men. Except my body and my mind. They can't have either.

12. How do you feel about the prison system or the justice system?

I was given a 50 to life sentence for three strikes burglary. Murderers, rapists, and child molesters still get less time.

13. What makes you laugh?

Corny jokes.

14. Finish the sentence:

If I could change the world, I would put paper bags on everyone. When we can't see who a person is, then you don't know what gender, race, or religion someone is. But take the bags off and we have a fear because it is what people are taught. So I would change the world by conversation.

I believe that we aren't defined by what we are, but who we are.

I wish that everyone could see what I see through these blue eyes—I see love, hope, faith, tolerance, and acceptance every day.

I am inspired by Rosa Parks and how alone she must have felt on that bus but still, as a black woman, had the courage to make a difference. So as a white trans woman in a men's prison that is alone, I still have the courage to make a difference.

15. Please share anything else you'd like. This is your space. And your voice.

As a trans woman in a men's prison, I am looked passed because I am smart, funny, beautiful, and have red hair. So every time I walk into a room, I make sure that I own it. So if I walk in the room everyday, then it always is as if it's the first time.

Being who you say you are is so important in this world. We have to embrace each other for not just what we see but for what is inside, and we must value friendships and lives—not to take this life for granted. The children of this world need to be inspired by adults and told that their lives matter each day. Without the children to thrive, we have nothing. We can all be better if we try a little harder.

Lisa Strawn

P.S. You can find more of my writing on Prison Radio.

July 3, 2018

Lisa,

I have been blessed with you because not only have I read your words, but I have heard your voice. I am grateful that you passed along your work on Prison Radio, and I am grateful to Prison Radio for creating the platform. The first I heard your voice was reciting Assata Shakur's "Affirmation," and I felt the life in it: "I believe that seeds grow into sprouts. And sprouts grow into trees...I believe in living. I believe in birth. I believe in the sweat of love and in the fire of truth."

And then I clicked on your own creation, "Struggle to Survival." Your words and your voice made the truth of my life and every advocate's life—of humanity—crystal clear: "The only way to make a difference," you said, "is to be different." To that, I say a long, "Mmmm," a yes that vibrates from my soul.

And then I clicked on Prison Radio's homepage and found, just a short scroll down, a photo of Alice Walker, who is listed as the sole supporter under "Endorsements," and whose words seem to grace the website. I will not make you listen to the whole story, just know that Alice Walker, though we've never met, is very special to me. It is her words that came to me and reminded me, at age 16 and then again and again in the last 12 years, that I want to be a writer—that it calls to me. I did not know that she was such an involved advocate for people who are incarcerated, but this does not surprise me; she is a woman so free in her spirit that she cannot help but recognize the freedom in others, in their spirits even if they're confined behind bars. She has always been an advocate for the oppressed.

This is all to say thank you. Thank you for sharing your voice with me through my project. I appreciate your courage and your honesty and your spirit. And thank you for awakening the synchronicities in my life, for being one of them. You remind me that spirit is at work within us and between us.

What I wonder is how you remain so hopeful, so certain that "love, hope, faith, tolerance, and acceptance" exist. And that you find them and feel them everyday. Even your perception of the world seems daring and shows your unwillingness to quit. I admire you.

I also admire the way you declare every part of you, refusing to deny who you are: "I like everything about me," you wrote. "I would not change a thing."

In solidarity,
Ashley

Eric

Five.

April 15, 2018

Eric,

I read your writing on Adopt an Inmate's blog a while ago, specifically your discussions on *The Four Agreements*. Ever since I read your series, you've come across my mind: I am impressed by the way you write and your desire to share secrets to wellbeing with others.

And, so, as I am a writer who has begun to embark on a new project meant to share and celebrate the voices of individuals who are incarcerated, I'm glad I have kept you in mind.

My purpose for writing this letter is to tell you about this book project I'd like to pursue and to invite you to join me in it.

I've enclosed a "Share Your Voice" sheet for you with more information. I would be honored if you want to participate and share your answers to some or all of the questions.

Whether you choose to participate or not, I am grateful that you continue to share your voice with the world through your writing.

Kind regards,
Ashley

April 22, 2018

Ashley—

Hey! So I received your note and questions. I plan to answer all the questions, but I wanted to shoot you a short note back letting you know I'm interested in participating in your project. I would, however, like a copy of the book when it's completed. :)

So, obviously you've read my profile, but I'd like you to know a few things. I'm not into head games. I'm not out to ask for things. I'm not out for or into shady dealings, you know. I know a lot of guys in here who are, and they give us regular guys a bad rap. I just wanted to say that!

I'm glad you liked my blogs. I believe there are two new ones recently posted. I do enjoy writing them, but a couple things hold me back. First, I'm always under a time crunch with school and different things on which I'm working—it's the irony of my life, right? I'm doing time but don't have any time.

And, second, it's sometimes difficult to find adequate subjects on which to write. I mean, I'm not into writing about the bad food or other petty things. I get perhaps my petty is not the same as another's, but personally, I'm into deeper waters, ya know what I mean?

As far as my schooling, I'm currently in my second course for my Ph.D. program, all the while doing research for my dissertation, which, honestly, is the most intimidating project I've attempted in my history of ever! But my 62 text reference list *and* topic *and* title was all approved by the board at the university. So ain't nothin' to it but to do it now.

Yoga, huh? I've never tried it, but they actually have a yoga class here. A couple cats have encouraged me to go. I haven't yet.

Anyway, I just wanted to say hello and let you know I'm interested in your project. If you feel like hittin' me back and starting a conversation, I wouldn't mind. I'm always open to talking with interesting people.

With respect,
E. Burnham

April 29, 2018

Hi Eric,

Thanks so much for writing back and for taking the time to answer my questions. I appreciate that! And, of course, I will make sure the final copy of the book gets into your hands.

I'm impressed by your academic ambitions! I'd love to know: what are you writing your dissertation on? I have my undergraduate degree in English, so I've written two theses, but never a dissertation. I wrote my first thesis on Virginia Woolf's novel *Mrs. Dalloway* (my favorite!) about time and whether it exists. Her writing makes me feel like time past, present, and future are all one, all here now.

On a completely different note, I guess I'll tell you about my day. I'm writing to you on Sunday morning. When I finish this, I will probably do some yoga and then I'm off to the car dealership to get a new car! I bought my first car 11 years ago, when I was in high school, and it has carried me around faithfully for all these years. So, for that, I'm grateful. But it's time for something new. I'm not very much into cars, but this new step with a new car is giving me a small burst of excitement, gratitude, and pride.

This week is unusually eventful for me. On Friday night, I'm leading a workshop called "The Ugly Side of the Beauty Industry" about the often toxic chemicals found in skincare products. And Saturday morning is the Book Launch Party for my new book, *The Moon and Her Sisters.*

So, to end, I'll share with you a couple of poems from that new book. The first is the poem which opens my book and from where the book gets its name, and the second is one of my favorites.

The first:

Not everyday will you feel like the moon,
silvery, defiant, always becoming.
But I think you and the moon
come from the same mother
because within you is the power to
wane and wax,
unleashing all seasons of you,
and with this comes the innate force to light up
your body from within
until you just can't stop it and—look
they can see it, too.

—*the moon and her sisters*

The second:

I think you're going to gather me.
You won't see me across the room
and be struck by me.
No,
I think you'll squint your eyes,
intrigued by me
and I will wash over you
slowly.
There will be
no shouting, no racing,
no awe-inducing moment
to begin our romance

because I reveal myself
quietly
and only those who have the eyes
to notice
will capture it.
Let me tell you:
when you do discover me,
I come powerfully—
like the shadow cast by the moon
during an eclipse:
I will deluge you.
But it is a gentle intensity,
swallowing you
in your wholeness and
lifting you up.
I am telling you:
once you know,
there will be fire raging
up your spine,
behind your heart—
You want her,
it will say.
Go get her.

In friendship,
Ashley

May 5, 2018

Ashley—

Hey you! It was really nice to receive your letter! I wasn't sure if you'd write, but I *am* glad you did. And answers to your questions will be coming, posthaste. See, I have set aside the whole day tomorrow to answer your questions. So, we're basically spending the day tomorrow hangin' out. I figure you order the pizza and I'll bring the soda? Or you could make a veggie pizza if you're a vegan.

So how is you new car? Are you flying around corners, hugging the road, down shifting as you enter the heart of the curve in order to allow the increase in RPMs to slow you down enough to maintain grip—barely in control, just before you upshift again and floor it out of the curve, darting smoothly around the slower cars? Or are you babying the new ride, keeping it under 55 mph?

Oh, oh, I forgot to answer your question about my dissertation: the title is "Understanding the Biopsychosocial-spiritual Aspects of Homosexuality in Counseling." I have 62 sources in my bibliography, which I had to have pre-approved by the board at the University before I could even begin.

So how did your workshop go? I'm sure there are an unimaginable number of toxic chemicals in so-called skincare products. I read a study in which sample groups from each geographical region of the country were tested —ultimately around 9,500 people in all. The results showed that the average American has over 80+ industrial chemicals in their blood. It was wild.

Oh, and how did your Book Launch Party go? Did you autograph around 1000 copies for your adoring fans? And you said, "My *new* book." So how many books have you published? Am I corresponding with a famous author? Like, have you had lunch with the Queen? Does she text you in the middle of meetings with high-brow jokes and astute observations? Anyway, I'd love to read your book —I cannot receive it in the mail from you, but I can receive any book directly from Amazon.

So I dig your poems. I've never been too much into poetry, primarily because I've never been motivated, save the "Roses are red; violets are blue" poems in middle school in cards to cute girls. ;) I'm always into reading *your* poetry and poems you like. I'm a big quotes guy, so I'll leave you with two of my favorites:

"There is a difference between knowing the path and walking the path."
—Morpheus

"Everyone is broken by life, but some people are stronger in the broken places."
—Ernest Hemingway

Your new friend,
Eric

May 6, 2018

Ashley—

Hey! So here are the first eight questions; I just wanted to show you that I'm serious. Next weekend, I will answer the remaining seven and mail them out.

I hope you're doing well.

Eric

1. Introduce yourself! Tell me a little about you:

My name is Eric, but most people in my world call me Burn-One. I'm known to society as inmate #12729124. I turned 39 years old on April 21, 2018. I was 21-years-old when I was convicted of murder, and I have now spent 42.7 percent of my life behind bars. I basically grew up in prison.

I take full responsibility for the actions that brought me to prison, and I don't labor under the misconception that I don't deserve to be here. I took another man's life during a physical altercation. He and I had a disagreement over a prior circumstance. We fought and, unfortunately, I walked away and he did not. I'm deeply ashamed of not only how my actions hurt someone else, but also the man I was, my self-concept that made such an action acceptable in my mind. I feel profoundly guilt-stricken, as, of course, I should. I think about it literally every day, but I'm not the same person today that I was then.

I've worked extremely hard to become a better man, a man who could positively contribute to society if given the chance. I've increased my education, earning a B.A. in Counseling in 2015, an M.C.C. in Counseling in 2017, and I'm currently enrolled in a Ph.D. program. Yet, my education is not all I have worked on.

I've increased my empathy for others through self-awareness. I've learned that others are just as important as me, and I'm more like other people than I am different from them. I don't feel entitled to anything from anyone, and I've gotten in touch with the deepest part of myself in order to understand both my purpose for being and how to realize it. But perhaps most importantly, I've learned what it means to be a good person and, while I'm certainly not perfect, I strive to live up to that each day.

A long time ago (roughly 2005), I learned a valuable life lesson from a very bad person. See, I was in a four man cell, and one of the guys assigned to that cell with me was one of those guys with whom everyone has a problem. Each and every day, he and I had a mild-to-moderate confrontation. Whenever he would leave, although nobody spoke of it, we all felt a deep sense of calm. When he would return, he would inevitably bring tension and chaos with him. From this I realized that I don't want that for my life. I don't want life to get better for anyone because I left the room. I want life to be better for people because I was in the room, at least as much as it is up to me. I think that's the most important thing anyone should know about me.

2. Describe what you look like. What do you like about how you look? Is there something you wish you could change?

Picture this suave, sexy, electrifying cat. Okay, you got that picture in your mind? Okay, now realize I'm probably nothing like what you've pictured. I'm 5'9" and 185 lbs, mildly athletic build, shaved head, and a goatee. In the summertime, I do grow tan. I have deep laugh lines because I do laugh easily. I'm relatively attractive, but nothing special, a hard average. I do have a lot of bad tattoos, and I regret those. If and when I get released, I will have many of them either fixed or removed. I like to think my personality makes up for whatever I lack physically.

3. Do you have family? If so, tell me about them.

I was raised by a single mother who struggled with an amphetamine addiction while I was growing up. I love my mother, and I know she did the best she could with what she had. I don't hold anything against her. She taught me respect and instilled a solid work ethic in me. My mom is also a very generous woman. She was in a car accident and received a settlement. It was with some of that money that she paid for my education, giving me an opportunity the vast majority of other incarcerated people do not have. I'm extremely grateful to her for that, and I'm grateful for all she went through raising me and my sister while working out her own issues.

My sister is five years older than me, and although we are in touch, unfortunately we are not close. I know much about her life, but I don't know her very well. I would like to, however.

My mother and sister are not doing well. This week I found out my mother is in the hospital with congestive heart failure, and my sister has cancer. The doctors say she has five good years left. The most heart-wrenching part is that because of the actions of my youth, I am unable to be there for my family. I would give anything to be there with them.

4. Do you have children? If so, what do you most love about them? What do you miss about them?

I have no children, but I do hope to have a child one day. I do not know if I will be given the privilege, however.

5. What are your goals?

My goals are ultimately to make a positive impact on the world, whether in here or out. I want to use my education and insights to help others who struggle. Every human being makes a ripple in the pond of life. I want mine to somehow improve the pond, and I have a lot of work left to do.

6. If you could leave prison for a day, what would you do?

Hmm, I know I would, without question, see if my time outside of these walls could somehow allow me to help my family with something. Other than that, perhaps I would enjoy a good meal that isn't prison food. But a day outside of prison may give me sensory overload. I came to prison prior to 9/11, so the world is so much different, so much faster. There is literally too much to see and do for one day. Whatever I would do, I'd do it with my family.

7. Do you believe your life has a purpose or specific mission? What is it?

I do think there is a reason for why things happen, but I don't buy into a deterministic reality where we have little choice. As a human being, I feel I have a general purpose to learn, to grow, and to edify my fellow human beings when I can. In a more specific sense, I'm convinced I am called to use my experiences and opportunities to help others who struggle with the same types of things I have. Life is difficult for everyone, and I believe the Creator orchestrates things in such a way that human brokenness becomes valuable when it's used to help others.

8. What do you think makes a good friend?

A good friend is someone with whom you can be yourself and still be comfortable, someone with whom you can laugh and cry. When you need help, a good friend is there, he or she is loyal and authentic, with no hidden agendas or ulterior motives. Yet a good friend will challenge you when it's needed, willing to tell you hard truths, and will allow you to challenge him or her when it's needed as well. The most beneficial relationships are reciprocal and deep friendships must be.

May 20, 2018

Hi Eric,

Thanks so much for your letter *and* your first set of answers to my questions! I'm glad we got to spend the day together metaphorically. You're right—I'm a vegan so, if it were up to me, I'd definitely bring the veggie pizza to our hangout.

Yes, I'm enjoying my new car. It's got new features (well, new to me, at least) like, for the first time, I don't need a key to turn on the ignition. It hooks up to my phone so I can make and receive calls from my car and I can connect my music to it (gone are the days of CD players in cars). But I'm certainly not as cool as you! I love how you describe driving a car; it's like I can feel you hugging the curves, flying around corners. I'm 28 years old, but I tease I drive like an old woman—safe, cautious. But now that the weather is finally in an upward swing, I do like rolling the windows down and letting the wind ride through my hair. My friend Caitlyn teases that my car looks like a sexy man, so she's named my car "Rafael."

I've written two books (only a few months apart. The first I published in January, the second in April of this year), but famous author is a bit of a stretch! I'm not tight with the Queen or Oprah…yet. My book launch party was beautiful; I felt like I was riding the wave of its energy for days. I felt so nourished by all the people who showed up to support me and listen to me read. There were even several little girls (all under 9 years old) who sat patiently, quietly, and kindly as I read. That was a blessing. What I don't think I told you is that I used the opportunity to share the words of some of the women I write to who are incarcerated. I read the audience a poem I had written about alternatives to mass incarceration and then said that I'm lucky to be able to express my voice in this way, but not everyone has the opportunity I do. And, so, I took a few sentences from my pen pals' letters to me (with their permission) and read them aloud. One quote was from my friend Britney, who is in a Texas prison, and she wrote about war and how love is the only answer, the only truth. I look forward to collaborating with you more in the future and getting to share your words alongside mine and other's.

Speaking of quotes, thanks for the ones you shared with me. You included one from Ernest Hemingway who, when I was in high school, was one of my favorite writers. I read his book *Farewell to Arms* and remember being mesmerized by the way he wrote: he was so strict and efficient with his words, as if he couldn't allow any gratuitous words to slip into his writing. His book hung heavy around me (it was, after all, about war) and conveyed the nothingness of war through his minimal, almost empty language.

You say you didn't like literature class but you are a fantastic writer! Your answers to my questions are thoughtful, contemplative, and even funny. (I can tell you have a good sense of humor.) Your goals to make a positive impact on the world are powerful and bold and I know you are already on that path. I'm grateful for the way you've already impacted my life.

I will end by telling you about the movie I saw last night. It was called *Pope Francis: A Man of His Word*. I am spiritual, not religious, but I felt called to see this film because Pope Francis has been an outlier, using his position to call for progressive change for our planet and for all people no matter how rich or how poor. The film showed him speaking at several prisons in the United States and he said, "If God forgets the mistakes someone makes in his past, then who am I not to? Not forgetting, then, is a sin." We are all seen and loved equally by god.

I just ordered my book *The Moon and Her Sisters* for you. Amazon says it should arrive by May 23rd, which means it may even arrive before this letter!

In friendship,
Ashley

May 14, 2018

Share Your Voice questions continued:

9. What's your biggest life lesson so far?

I think the biggest life lesson I've learned is that I'm more like all the people I do not like than I'm different from them. We are all human, and we are all struggling through this life as best we can. Some of us are more broken by life than others, but we are really all the same inside. So, given that we are all more alike than we are different, I can't judge anyone, and I can't dogmatically evaluate others based on their ability to overcome human brokenness; or their failure to overcome their own.

10. What advice would you give to your younger self or to a child in a similar position as you were when you were young?

I think I would say, be genuine. The vulnerability of authenticity is cathartic, allowing for pent up fears, insecurities, and irrational perceptions of reality to be released in profoundly subtle but extremely important ways. See, fear, insecurity, and irrational perceptions of reality only have power when kept in the dark. When behind a mask, they can deceive us into thinking they will manifest in the worst possible way, to expose whatever it is we wish to be kept hidden. Yet, when they are brought into the light, they lose all power because they are shown to have *only* the influence given to them. Without a mask, they have no power at all.

11. What does it feel like to live in prison?

I think the answer depends upon in what phase of incarceration a person is asked. Early on, it is frightening and painfully lonely. As time passes, one gets comfortable, accustomed to routine, even dependent upon it. More time passes, one begins to lament a life wasted. Mostly, prison hurts not so much because I'm locked away from everything I knew for so long that everyone I once knew doesn't know me anymore, but because, deep down, I deserve it. While I do not belong here, I certainly deserve to be here.

12. How do you feel about the prison system or the justice system?

I feel it is broken. I feel it is unfair on several different levels. The wealthy are treated differently than the poor at every phase of the criminal justice process. The incarcerated are caged like animals, treated as if they're irredeemably nefarious and hopelessly opportunistic. The staff who run prison facilities are often maliciously punitive in their application of rules and regulations. Even those staff members who see the mistreatment and feel uneasy about it are often forced to go with the flow of "how things are" or face being ostracized; therefore, they remain complicit in the politics of oppression.

Rehabilitation is literally a politician's term. The incarcerated individual is certainly not pushed toward change. He or she is steeped in rage. If one achieves change, it is only because he or she clawed up the mountain with very little help from the system.

If one does not know how to change, he or she is defined
by that inability, rather than taught how or why it's
important. The criminal justice system in the United
States is broken.

13. What makes you laugh?

Intelligent people making unforced observations about
the world's imperfections; children playing; or my friends
laughing—that is contagious. I'm very playful and I laugh
quite easily. Simple things make me laugh, but I do not
like casual cruelty. I don't laugh at others' weaknesses or
failures.

14. Finish the sentence:
If I could change the world, I would work to repair an
economic system in the U.S. that leaves 50 million people
in poverty while the mutual fund and stockpiled wealth of
Fortune 500 companies grows to over 15 trillion dollars
(2016 numbers). I would structure a system favorable to
business while less exploitative to primary social
relationships, such as the nuclear and extended family. I
would seek to scale back the commodification of the
individual and facilitate a cultural shift toward the
education of everyone. A tall order, I know, but the
premise was if I *could* change the world, right?

I believe that every single person on the planet has
intrinsic worth. They only need an opportunity to show it.

I wish my family could be ok. I wish they could be
healthy and happy, and I wish I could be with them, even
if only for a little while.

I am inspired by hard working underdogs. When someone makes their way back from the bottom to the top through purely hard work, that is definitely inspirational.

15. Please share anything else you'd like. This is your space. And your voice.

I have a blog I'd like to share for question #15:

Good Enough
by Eric Burnham

Human brokenness is a universal aspect of the human experience, right? I mean, we are all messed up a little. It's the common denominator that links us all and levels the playing field to a certain extent. There are countless variations, but we all feel it with great depth, each one of us. The great American poet Ernest Hemingway wrote, "The world breaks everyone and afterward many are strong at the broken places." That is a simple yet profound way to frame the human condition, but it leads to so many questions, especially for the incarcerated.

Are the strong those who have never allowed their own brokenness to harm others? Or are they those who overcome their own brokenness despite having harmed others? One cannot come to prison for taking a human life without being broken mentally, emotionally, and spiritually, and I don't mean broken as an effect of incarceration. I mean broken as the cause of my violence, the very impetus for my horrible crime. The depth and reach of the type of brokenness required to take another man's life during a physical altercation in which I was the aggressor must be pervasive and complete, leading me to wonder...*does my brokenness break me?* Am I so psychologically disintegrated that I'm incapable of truly overcoming my brand of brokenness in order to move forward and effectually impact the world in a positive way?

Of course, some broken things retain a degree of functionality, still able to do some good. Most people have heard the proverb about the woman with the cracked pot. The pot was depressed because it was unable to hold water. It slowly leaked as the woman walked home from the local well each day, and constantly compared itself to the pot the woman carried in her other hand which did not leak. One day, the leaky pot said to the woman, "You should discard me and get a new pot that functions as it was designed, like your other one."

She responded to her broken pot, saying, "I've been aware of your flaw these many years, and I've used it to my advantage. Notice along your side of the path the abundance of flowers blooming in this desert, which could not be watered properly if you did not leak so perfectly." The leaky pot looked and saw the beautiful variety of flowers along only one side of the path, the side on which it was carried, and was astonished. From that point forward, that leaky pot never felt insecure again.

On the other hand, that story, while comforting, remains somewhat of a fairy tale. Most broken things are discarded in favor of fully functional new things, things that function as they were designed. Household appliances, car parts, phones, these are all things that are quickly replaced when they cease to function optimally.

Yet, I am not a thing. Things are simple. I'm a complex human being, and for the first 23 years of my life, my brokenness manifested in ways that hurt others and negatively impacted my environment. I spread darkness, decay, and pain through my self-centeredness. The question that haunts me is…*can a bad person become good?*

However, I remain a man who took a life in anger. I'll never be able to change that. A character that Ben Affleck played in a movie, Doug McRay, said, "No matter how much you change, you still gotta pay a price for the things you've done. So, I got a long way to go." I connect with that sentiment so deeply, and I cannot help but lament the possibility that my past may disqualify me from ever being a good man.

I've worked extremely hard to become a better person, to achieve balance and reciprocation in my relationships, to appreciate and even celebrate the differences between myself and others. I've grown into a man who cares about the humanity and dignity of others, who understands that I'm not entitled to special treatment or to violate the rights of others in order to meet my own needs. I've learned the value of working hard to earn something and waiting my turn because I'm not more important than anyone else. I've increased my education level, my capacity for critical thinking, logical reasoning, and associative thought, my emotional control, and my spiritual understanding.

A good man is authentic, trustworthy, and loyal. He does not seek accolades. He helps others easily, and avoids doing harm whenever possible. He is reliable, honorable, and strong-minded. He is humble, caring, and teachable. He operates with integrity, carries himself with dignity, and treats others with kindness. He pushes back when pushed too far, but never looks for trouble. He stands up for the helpless, but understands when to remain seated. And perhaps most importantly, he takes responsibility for his actions, admits his mistakes, and offers a genuine apology when necessary.

I sincerely strive to uphold these ideals every day. Yet I fall short more often than I'd like, and I worry it's because I'm irreparably damaged. I mean, it's not just the fact that my violence removed another human being from this planet that is deplorable; it is the fact that I was capable of such an act.

I have been incarcerated for 18 years for something I did when I was 21-years-old, but I honestly do not believe I have paid for what I've done. How can I quantify the value of a human life? Was he worth 25 years? 50? I can *never* pay for the life I took. All I can do is use the actions of my past to shape the direction of my future. I can do my absolute best to make sure I strive to be a good man, readily admit when I've made a mistake, and purposely impact others positively, in one way or another, every single day. But I'm not sure it's good enough.

Personal growth, to me, means becoming the person I was designed to be. I'm not too sure where the balance is found between nature and nurture in the formation of my spirit as a unique human being. I do know, however, that I'm just one incarcerated man trying to overcome my past mistakes and make a positive impact on this crazy world. I kind of think that's what life is all about: taking the bad and using it for good.

May 28, 2018

Eric,

I was listening last night to an interview from a couple years ago with actor Chris Pine. He was talking about sinking into the present—that doing that is, essentially, his mission especially in situations that may feel inauthentic or unnatural like photoshoots or giving interviews or acting—pretending a fake story is real while contending with a camera in your face. And he talked about how, by sinking into the present, he can simply allow what's meant to be to unfold without needing to control it (or without the assumption that it's even in his control).

What I love about your responses to my questions is that you also seem to sink into them. Your letters to me feel different: in them, you are funny, cool, like you've written with a cadence—it's like in your words you've dropped a beat. Your responses to my questions, though, drop into something else, an ulterior present that is reflective and I keep using the word "sunken" because it's like you've dropped into your body or maybe deeper, into the collective soul of us and the earth.

This is not to say that one way of writing is better than the other: in fact, what I most admire about you is that you hold all of these ways of being and expressing yourself within you, which is the truth of who we are. We are not singular.

And I mentioned Chris Pine at the beginning because I think you're saying something similar: you set yourself free by dropping into the present moment and releasing everything else. As you put it, "The vulnerability of authenticity is cathartic, allowing for pent up fears, insecurities, and irrational perceptions of reality to be released in profoundly subtle but extremely important ways."

I share this also because both your writing and Chris Pine's words in that interview feel acutely relevant to me right now. I've been writing and speaking more publicly lately about my search for "my man," my partner. And what I'm coming to discover is that I cannot find him if I keep up any artifice, if I try to make myself more palatable at the expense of expressing my truth, and I do not want to attract someone held back by the fear of living in the present, of dropping into it and riding it with me.

You wrote about the vicious cycle of trying to keep hidden parts of ourselves, and I want someone willing to expose it all with me and with others and with life, to break free.

I think one of the blessings of getting to write letters to anyone is that they become a space to work out and share our feelings. They are intimate in that way—more profound expressions that we often don't share with each other in everyday life. I think what comes out in letters is too often a lost intimacy, something that swiping to someone's photo on a dating app on your phone or texting or the general disconnection we have from our groundings—each other and the earth—can't provide.

We need a change.

This is all to say thank you. My mission, when I started writing these letters to people who are incarcerated, was to let them know that I hear them—that they are seen, recognized. But, as is clear here, the seeing and the hearing goes both ways.

I had a tinge of hesitancy in sending this to you because it is exposure and maybe it'll be misconstrued—or I'll be misconstrued or judged or that something will be irrevocably changed. But then I remembered: exposure is everything I've been seeking.

Thanks for letting me break free. I feel like, with each inch and with this letter and with Chris Pine's words and all the letters from all the people in prisons across this country that have been filling my mailbox lately, I am closer to finding him—and finding myself.

Please continue to write (in all your styles!). I look forward to our continued friendship.

Kindly,
Ashley

Eric didn't receive my letter from May 28th before sending me the following note. So it has become a running joke between us, of whether we're "in sync" or not. He and I will play a bit of catch up in the proceeding letters.

May 26, 2018

Ashley—

How's my favorite New Yorker? Seriously, it's nice to hear from you again, and I received your book! Thank you! I've read some of it. I'm going to read it all.

Ha! What do you mean you're not as cool as me? I'm just a former gangster who has turned his life around, a bad guy who became a good guy—same 'ole story. Everybody's heard it before. But you, you're a hip, young New Yorker (we'll work on how to jazz up the description of how you drive!).

Hmm, your friend Caitlyn sounds like she knows how cool you are, too. I mean, she named your car "Rafael." So, I mean, you're pretty cool. It isn't fair, though. You know what I look like, but I don't know what either you or your sexy side-kick Rafael look like. I'd love a picture.

So you're not tight with the Queen or Oprah? Well perhaps just Rachel Ray and Michelle Obama then? I feel like you travel with a high brow crowd, no? The liberal fashion crowd who writes books, flies back and forth from NY to LA in between talk show interviews promoting your business, all the while combatting social justice. Hmm, or perhaps you're the brooding poet, ever the recluse, primarily because you see the world more completely than most and every time you try to explain your worldview to others, they look at you like you're insane? ;)

I love the self-awareness you displayed when you wrote, "I felt so nourished by all the people who showed up to support me and listen to me read." I've gotta say, that shows an uncommon degree of emotional intelligence for 28. I mean, I know I've been in prison for a long time (since you were 10 years old), and my frame of reference is incarcerated men, it still seems like you may have one of those "old soul" personalities.

Thank you for your kind words about my writing. As an educated prisoner, writing is my primary tool for self-expression, a tool that is unavailable to many in here because they lack the education or motivation to use it, which is sad.

I have not seen the Pope Francis movie you mentioned, but I do agree with the quote you included. I think if God has gone to the lengths He has to make forgiveness available, then who are we to not forgive others and give them every opportunity to succeed?

Well, I certainly am fond of your letters and I do look forward to hearing from you again. I'm interested in learning more about my new friend. Until then, don't forget to smile today.

Friendship back at ya,
E. Burnham

June 4, 2018

Ashley—

Hey you! I really enjoy your letters. I think what I dig the most is that our conversations are genuine, unforced, and free-flowing. There aren't any presuppositions or even boundaries, save those of cordiality, civility, and the reciprocation of respect. I would like to alleviate your uncertainty regarding your "exposure."

First of all, you do not need to fret in the least about being misunderstood or that I would, in any way, misconstrue your words. I will never read something into them or take either the written content or the underlying emotion of your letters in a way you did not intend. I am a *very* communication-oriented man, so if I'm unclear, I will simply ask you. I'm also assertive enough to express my own thoughts in ways that do not wrestle away the microphone.

Second, I *in no way* will ever judge you—especially when you are opening up to me. We are all so fragile, and our natural personalities and emotional temperaments are shaped by our personal experiences and the environments in which we reach individualized developmental milestones. Consequently, we are all unique in a multitude of ways while remaining exquisitely similar in fundamental ways, leaving us more the same than we are different, and it is precisely this truth that should lead us all to a greater degree of not only acceptance and tolerance, but also compassion, mercy, and grace to embrace all the pleasant distinctions among us as a people. So you can be as open and honest with me as you like. I both appreciate and enjoy the sincerity of your thoughts. I promise to treat them with the care and dignity they deserve. No judgments here—I pinky swear!

Okay, now that I got the important stuff said, I can move on to your wonderful letter. Man, I just realized I've inserted my foot deep into my mouth by implying the rest of what I have to say is somehow less important. I assure you—that is not the case. I'm just a guy, so...I say dumb stuff from time to time. Please forgive me.

Thank you for your kind words about both my letters and my responses to your questions. I'm glad you enjoy them. I, too, enjoy your letters. My tail does wag a bit when I see your name on the return address.

I've never heard of Chris Pine, but it sounds as if I'd like him, or at least his philosophical interpretation of the present. I feel strongly about "being here now." I'm convinced I cannot become the man I want to be—kind, genuine, thoughtful, honest, good—without being all those things presently, purposively, and perpetually.

I agree with you—we are not singular. We all have so much inside of us, you know, but Western cultural norms seem to encourage this compartmentalization of the self, having us hide or "square away" that which isn't for public consumption. Unfortunately, it works to fragment the aspects of the soul that make us who we are. I mean, of course I'm not saying we should all strip down to our underwear, sit down at a park bench, and tell the weird homeless guy our deepest fears or secrets. I'm just saying the very ethos of social relationships in our culture involves civilized dishonesty—we all work to conform to the ethos, rather than allowing the ethos to be a collective expression of who we *really* are, you know?

What?!? You think I'm cool, funny (wag, wag, wag). Well, now I'm all blushing and stuttering. No, I'm playing. I'm just myself. I'm the same way in letters as I am in real life. I'm a "thinker" type, but I also have a "doer" personality —and I'm always handy with a joke. I can make almost anyone laugh. If I can't make someone laugh, they have no soul. They're a vampire or something. :)

Yeah, I guess that's real. I do set myself free by "dropping into the present moment and releasing everything else." I think the vulnerability of authenticity keeps us grounded. When we wear a mask, even if it's only the mask of cultural ethos described earlier, some of the self is lost, primarily because it wasn't meant to be hidden, which ultimately hurts us inside. It sounds cliché, but it remains true: we were meant to live, not merely exist. And we live now. We breathe now. We love now. We can waste a lot of time worrying about wasted time, no?

I do totally agree with you, Ashley. You'll never find your partner if you aren't willing to be real, to be congruent, because when you operate with incongruence of self, you'll only attract others (potential partners) who are incongruent themselves. The incongruent are threatened by the congruent, so if you are willing to be all that you are—the perfectly imperfect specimen of humanity that you are, then you'll unconsciously avoid, even repel, the soulmate you seek.

I feel like the universe is funny that way. We all have these frog warts we are desperately afraid of others seeing, right, but the wild part is those frog warts—and how we deal with and respond to our warts—is what ultimately makes us who we are. And if we will just accept ourselves as we are, we could be the beautiful creatures we were designed to be. And wonder of all wonders, when we pull off the mask and let others see our real warts, we can find the one that not only falls in love with our warts, but we find we can truly love theirs as well.

Yeah, letters can be intimate, I agree. I also enjoy conversations, too. Although I haven't had one like this in YEARS, these are wonderful conversations to have in real life, too, I'm sure. I feel like this would be a cool conversation to have over some veggie nachos, no?

Haha! You said the conversations in letters are more intimate than swiping someone's picture on a dating app. Well, I've never swiped anyone's picture on a dating app. I've never even been on Facebook. In fact, to "swipe" a pic used to mean to steal it.

Aw, nothing will be "irrevocably changed" by being open and honest. Who knows, we could end up being close friends—deep connections form in fundamentally unorthodox ways in postmodern society. So I look forward to our continued friendship as well (wag, wag, wag). I do look forward to hearing from you again. I'll leave you with some fun questions, okay?

1. Top 5 favorite character traits in a person?

2. Top 5 most-hated character traits in a person?

3. When is your birthday? Favorite color?

4. What do you do to relax when you're stressed?

5. Are you more introverted or extroverted?

Okay, I'll close. I don't want you to feel peppered. Until next time, don't forget to smile.

With much respect,
E. Burnham

June 7, 2018

Eric,

I think our letters are flying back and forth through the mail as we write to each other: meaning we're slightly out of sync lol. So I'm responding to the letter you wrote on May 26th. I have a feeling I may receive another one from you before you even receive this one. I was going to hold off to sync us back up again, but what the heck? We can follow along well enough.

And, mainly, I'm writing because you asked for a photo, so I'm going to deliver. As you said, it's only fair: I've seen yours! I don't have any photos of me and Rafael yet, but I'll work on that. For now, here are two of me: one in my favorite one-handed handstand with my fingers in a peace sign and the other, well, just as I am.

You're right—I would love to be friends with Michelle Obama. She's intelligent, articulate, witty, and compassionate. In fact, a couple years ago when I was seeking to fill my life with more nourishing and engaging friendships, a friend suggested I make a list of the type of women I'd like to imagine in my life. Her advice was based on the principle of manifestation and the law of attraction: I suppose she was saying that if I focus my energy by getting clear on the type of friends I'd like to have, it'll be easier to manifest. (I'm not entirely sure it works like that. Sometimes I feel the "positive thinking" paradigm is very privileged.) Still, I did it. At the top of my list was Michelle Obama along with Alice Walker, Malala Yousafzai, Emma Watson, and a few others. I'm still waiting on them. ;)

If you could choose any celebrity friends, who would you put on your list?

I like how perceptive you are: you're also right that I'm frequently described as an "old soul."

Thanks for reminding me to smile: often, it's just the reminder I need! Hope this letter brings you a little joy, too.

Till next time,
Ashley

At the top of this letter was a stamp, removed from the envelope I last sent to him, and re-placed here, on the letter he sent to me. The stamp says, "Love."

June 11, 2018

You put two of these stamps on your letter. So I sent one back—now I have one and you have one. Relax—I'm not makin' it weird. Friendship is a form of love, too, silly. :)

Ashley—

Hey you! It was such nice surprise to receive your letter tonight. And your pictures—wow! You are a stunning woman, but I'm sure you've heard that a whole bunch in your life. I will describe what I see in your photos in just a minute.

But, first, I will interact with your letter. I think I've grown quite fond of your letters, all without realizing it. It struck me how excited I felt when I got home from work at 4pm and your letter was sitting on my bed.

Haha! We're out of sync? Well it sure feels like *we* are in sync, even if our letters are not. Our new-found friendship seems to have taken off. I find you a very interesting person, and I love your conversational style of writing, although from time-to-time it feels as if you don't quite know what to say. But I do want you to know you can say whatever is on your mind or heart. You certainly aren't going to offend me or upset my "Western sensibilities." I'm extremely communication-oriented, so I will always comment on your thoughts. My thoughts on your thoughts—isn't that the elevated degree of intimacy of which you spoke in your last letter? I enjoy your thoughts on my thoughts, too, for the record.

Okay, to your pictures: I like your face. You seem to have expressive eyes. I bet it is interesting to watch you as you speak. Your smile is awesome, totally infectious, and I like the way your hair frames your very pleasant face.

As far as your handstand—WOW! That is tough! You are fit, huh? You've got a real "I'm a woman, and I'm a badass" thing goin' on. That's just too cool. Do you do yoga? Didn't you tell me you do? I'll have to read your other letters. I still have them all.

That would be cool if you could teach me yoga, but you'll have to bear with me. I've never done it. I'm an athlete—I played basketball, baseball, and football in high school and I still run, work out, and play basketball today. But yoga? I'm afraid I'd turn myself into a pretzel. I'm good, though. I can laugh at myself—even if a pretty woman is laughing at me.

Yeah, Michelle Obama does seem cool. I feel like President Obama seems cool, too. I feel like there are several strong-minded women I'd love to have lunch with, both liberal and conservative, lesbian and straight, all different ethnic and even national backgrounds. While I certainly have my own worldview and convictions, for sure, I enjoy very much learning how others see the world, how others experience life, and why they feel what they feel, think what they think, and do what they do.

Wow! I'm a fan of Malala Yousafzai, too. She's a badass, without question. I've read parts of her book and I watched an interview with her on late night television, Conan or something. She's amazing.

Yeah, that whole positive thinking *is* privileged, *so* much. I mean, sometimes life hurts; life can be lonely, difficult, even tragic. Putting on rose-colored glasses, denying reality, will never effectually impact the causes of—or even the experience of—pain. Yet there is something to optimistic thinking. I mean, always viewing the pizza as half gone is incredibly depressing, no? You still have half a pizza, and isn't it always better cold? (I'm assuming veggie pizza is the same?)

Okay, to your questions (wag, wag, wag):

If I could choose any celebrity friends, who would I put on my list? That's a tough one. So, my top 5:

Robert Downey, Jr. - I just love his story—prominent actor, heroin addiction, REAL prison time (not Martha Stewart time) and, finally, a tough climb back to the top. I dig that.

Van Jones - I really gained respect for him after Trump's election. He was livid on CNN. But then, he took the time to visit those in the Rust Belt who helped get Trump elected. While he may not agree, he took the time to listen to those with whom he disagrees—very respectable.

Kellyanne Conway - The first woman to EVER run a successful presidential campaign, for which she NEVER gets the credit she deserves, primarily because she's a conservative woman. She'd be amazing to converse with. I've seen many interviews—simply brilliant woman.

Tom Brady - I am a major football fan and I had the privilege of growing up watching Joe Montana play (yea, I know, total guy stuff). Now, Tom Brady has surpassed Joe Montana, so I'd love to talk football with him.

Dr. Drew - I'd love to geek-out on psychology and counseling with him. He is a brilliant man.

These, I think, are my top 5 of living celebrities. Who would you put in your top 5?

Aw, with a smile like yours, Ashley, you should smile *way* more often. Your face just lights up. I'm going to close this, but I do hope you are doing well. You should look yourself in the mirror, look yourself right in your eyes and say, "I am an amazing, strong, talented woman. I am unstoppable!" You should say that to yourself because it's true.

Okay, a couple questions:

1. Why are you a vegan?

2. What do you do when you cut loose and have fun?

3. What are your dreams, Ashley?

Ok, my new friend, I'm going to sleep. I look forward to hearing from you again, whether we're in sync or not!

With much respect,
Eric

June 19, 2018

Eric,

We're back in sync. ;)

I have to begin by saying that your blog post, "Good Enough," is so well-written. Reading it feels effortless and engaging and, like the best writing, new ideas arise when I read it. Thank you for sharing it with me. I'm also moved that you took the time to hand-write the entire post for me, something you've clearly already written and had to copy for my benefit. I see now that it's also posted on Adopt an Inmate's website. In the future, always feel free to ask me simply to check online first so you don't have to labor over rewriting. Know that I value the time and attention you've offered me.

I think the thing that most intrigues me is how you responded to my letter about seeking my partner. To borrow from "Good Enough," what touched me most is that you responded like a "good man." You listened intently and honored what I said, responding to it with care, respect, clarity, strength. I felt like I could trust you, and like you knew when to rise and advise and when to sit and listen.

In fact, it's like your personality rolls from you into these letters effortlessly. You have an admirable way of expressing yourself—clear and so easy for you that it's almost casual. I like it.

So let me answer your questions.

1. Top 5 favorite character traits in a person?
Hmm, good one. I love people who are articulate, who are passionate and follow their passions, who advocate for what they believe in, who are kind, and who are charismatic by the simple force of being who they are.

2. Top 5 most-hated character traits in a person?
Trump, I'm looking at you. ;)
I dislike someone who doesn't intend, advocate, or act in a way that spreads peace, and someone who uses age, gender, sexual orientation, ability, etc. to justify his or her belief that someone else is less or "other." I believe we need to spend more time, money, and attention teaching people not to act from anger (and showing them when they are and how to release it), because acting from pain does not make any of us better. And I dislike when someone preaches what they do not live. (That's only four, but it was a long four!)

3. When is your birthday? Favorite color?
January 31st. And I always used to say purple but, let's be honest, it's totally pink.

4. What do you do to relax when you're stressed?
I write to and connect with people like you. I work on projects I'm passionate about. I run or even simply take a walk outside.
I would like more people to fill more of the spaces of my life, to share joy and laughter.
And I'm not above watching Netflix.

5. Are you more introverted or extroverted?
Introverted, for sure.
However, put me in front of an audience to "perform"—to read my writing, speak, share, learn, and I light up.

Your turn. You have to answer 1-5, too!

Now let me respond to your second letter (playing catch up!). The fact that you thought to send me back one of my stamps was sweet and made me smile. Your humor about love was also much appreciated. (Wag)

You think I don't always know what to say to you, huh? Pssht, I'm never at a loss for words. ;) You've just got to ride my style, Eric. I'm more playful and open than my letters might insinuate. All good things take time, though. Let's keep writing and maybe you'll see the whole range of me. And, yes, I absolutely appreciate and welcome your thoughts on my thoughts. Bring it on.

So let's talk about your list of celebrity friends. I like that you chose Van Jones, a great advocate, especially for the systemic problems and deplorable public policy that has led to mass incarceration. But since you told me I won't offend your "Western civilities," we've got to talk about Kellyanne Conway. She may have helped Trump win the election, but I'd call his presidency and his candidacy (and his humanity) anything but successful. I don't doubt her political savvy. What I do doubt is her morality. I hope you enjoy your lunch with her, but I'd pass on that one. ;)

(And just to make sure that came across as I intended it in writing—I absolutely own and agree with everything I said about her, but I'm just playing with you. I appreciate you sharing honestly and don't want you to hold back!)

It seems this letter is turning into a book of its own. (This is what I get for trying to "sync" us up.) So let me do this with as much brevity as possible:

Who would I put in my top 5 celebrities I'd like to meet for lunch list?

I'm already worried that I'm going to leave someone out, so let me do it this way: these are the people who have been intriguing me the most lately, not necessarily a comprehensive list—

Hari Kondabolu, a comedian. I watched his most recent standup special on Netflix and actually laughed out loud through the whole thing. It was the first standup special in a while that I thought was genuinely funny—intelligent funny. Since then, I've been following him on Twitter and, to borrow your phraseology, wag my tail when he tweets not only jokes, but powerful commentary on social justice and current affairs.

Chris Pine, gotta add him after our last conversation. I'm curious what else he's got in his spirit and his mind.

Stephanie Devine, maybe not quite a celebrity but lunch-worthy to me. She's designing sustainable clothes, specifically the first zero-waste lingerie. The amount of clothing we use and discard is harming our planet and, therefore, our life force. Her mission is to create clothing that will literally disappear—biodegrade—without an impact on our earth. When you're done with it, you can simply bury it in your garden.

Matt Post, a recent high school graduate who has defied his youth and spoken courageously and powerfully about stricter gun laws.

Alice Walker, a writer and a classic. Have I written to you about her before? Her being and her writing continue to inspire me.

You have two more questions for me—why veganism? and what are my dreams? My favorite kinds of questions, thank you for them. I will save them for another letter for the sake of wrapping this one up.

Thanks for reminding me to smile. I hope you do, too.

In friendship and gratitude,
Ashley

June 21, 2018

Eric,

On this summer solstice as the planet turns and the seasons shift, I've decided to answer Part II, I'm calling it, of your questions.

Why veganism?

I feel like I've spent too much time using the word "vegan" to describe myself when, really, all I aim to be is someone who is mindful of what she puts in and on her body. Someone who considers her wellbeing, the wellbeing of her companion creatures—both animal and human, and the wellbeing of our planet. I don't think it's healthy or wise to so strictly define ourselves but, rather, to be moved by what our bodies tell us. I want to be an intuitive eater.

But eating more plants and less meat matters. We have, somehow, become complicit in raising a behemoth factory farming industry one that, like prisons, separates babies from their parents, locks life away in cages, and disappears (hides) its own cruelty. So well have we disappeared this industry that it's as if the food that sits on our plates is entirely separate from the death and pain it belies.

And I'm not saying that there may not, in nature, exist a food chain, where one creature's death fuels another's life —meaning where we are intended to use animals as our food. But I am certain there is a more compassionate and sacred way. I think we have only to look to our Native American friends and ancestors for that way.

The raising of animals for our food has also burgeoned into a monstrous use of our resources: we are destroying the planet in the process of trying to live off of meat. The planet gives us life: we come from it and we return to it. We cannot so callously disregard its health and longevity and expect to live well or live at all.

What are my dreams?

I have dreams for our planet and dreams for myself.

For our planet, I dream of peace, of course. Of a realization that we are linked—each of us and the earth. Our actions have broad and inextricable effects on our neighbors and on ourselves. What we do to one, we do to all.

For myself, I dream of independence, a fuller expression of who I am, of cresting—stepping into the glory of purpose magnified and great love.

I dream of writing more, speaking more, listening even more than I speak.

I dream of truer happiness, forever learning, and connections that wake my mind, body, and soul.

I dream of freedom within myself and in the way I move through the world.

I dream I am blessed to support myself by doing what I love and that I always crave to share what comes my way.

I dream not to leave a physical footprint on this earth, but a sense that, when I've left, there is even a glimmer more peace and more love.

Tell me your dreams, Eric. I want to know.

Ashley

I've decided to clip the final letter I'm including from Eric not to cut down his voice, but to amplify who he is to me: a man who is remarkably generous, present, funny, and self-aware. What I've noticed about him is that he's always willing to give—to buoy me with his words and to share, with deep reflection, his own self.

July 2, 2018

Ashley—

Hey you! I've been reading your book and wanted to share one of my favorite passages, this one:

I am seeking the man
who grows community gardens.
Not that he must put his hands
in the earth
and pray with the sun and the rain
for basil to grow—
no.
I am seeking the man
who knows that everything that
grows through him
and enters the world—
all of his words,
all of his actions,
all of his creations—
do not belong solely to him.
They will be collected
and eaten,
part of our becoming.

—what you feed the world matters

I like it, my friend. I also like your dreams. I, too, would like to see you fully actualized. I feel like it would be something to watch you fully blossom in self-discovery and self-expression, self-realization, and purpose fulfillment. I pray all your dreams come true. I mean, if your dreams come true, I think the world would necessarily be a better place.

What are my dreams?

My dreams, perhaps, are more selfish then yours, if I'm honest. I mean, I do have some altruistic tendencies. But much of that about which I dream has to do with proving to myself and the world that I'm worthy of participating in society, that I am not a vortex of selfishness, that I'm not a man who has chosen to meet my own needs at the expense of those around me. Although I made a horrible mistake and lived a lifestyle that harmed others, I am not irredeemable.

I dream of making a positive impact on the world. I dream of being a deeply good man, being filled with a love and compassion for others, motivated by my love for the Creator. I dream of using my education to help others.

I dream of freedom, of having a wonderful bond with a perfectly imperfect woman, of having a child and a family.

I dream of looking back on my life and knowing that I turned it around. I dream of loving deeply and pouring everything I have into everything I do. I suppose that is why I strive for honesty, integrity, and authenticity in my character. But, unfortunately, while this all sounds great, I do still fall short. I'm working on it.

Ashley, I love hearing from you and I hope you are doing well.

With a ton of respect,
Eric

Lacey

Six.

June 29, 2018

1. Introduce yourself! Tell me a little about you:

My name is Lacey Williams, TDCJ (Texas Department of Criminal Justice) calls me Lacey Watkins which is my ex-husband's name. I am 38 years old. I have lived a long, hard life. I have been abused all my life sexually, physically, mentally. I have lived in the country and the big cities. I am a countrified city girl. I was forced into prostitution after my crime. I have been threatened and my children have been threatened. I am now married to a God fearing man who is far from being abusive. God saved my life when he had me locked up.

2. Describe what you look like. What do you like about how you look? Is there something you wish you could change?

I am 5'5", white with dirty blonde hair. I weigh 180 lbs and I have hazel eyes. My hair is to the middle of my back. I love to smile and I believe my smile is the best part of me.

I have learned to love everything about me. Two years ago I would have said my height and weight. Not now.

3. Do you have family? If so, tell me about them.

I do have family. My blood family has pretty much disowned me because I am married to a black man and because of my crime. I have a younger sister that has three kids: two boys and a girl. My dad won't have anything to do with me, my mom is just as lost as I was at one time. My husband's family though loves me and accepts me for me. They treat me great and for the most part respect me.

4. Do you have children? If so, what do you most love about them? What do you miss about them?

I have two girls from my first marriage and my stepson now. I have not seen or talked to my girls in almost three years. My ex-husband will not let them have anything to do with me and my oldest, who will be 18 this year, is very hurt by the events that led to my incarceration. My oldest is Ashley. I love the fact that she always was smiling; she is my little twin. She always liked to snuggle and hug me all the time. My youngest daughter, Kody, she was very spunky. She would wrap her arms around my neck and squeeze so hard while she would wrap her legs around my waist. I miss those things about my girls.

My stepson acts just like his daddy, full of laughter and smiles. I miss that.

5. What are your goals?

My goals are to be a better mother and a better wife. To live a healthy, clean life full of God, love, and no abuse. To be a better daughter to my parents and a better sister.

6. If you could leave prison for a day, what would you do?

If I could leave prison for a day I would first go to my husband and then to my daughters and sit down with my girls and talk things out and work on reconciliation.

7. Do you believe your life has a purpose or specific mission? What is it?

I do believe my life has a purpose. I believe God has prepared me to help others with the same things that I have gone through.

8. What do you think makes a good friend?

A good friend to me is one that, no matter what you are going through—good, bad, or in between—that person is there. They love the lord. That person doesn't judge or step away. For me, that is my husband now, Kevin Williams. He has been my best friend for 25 years.

9. What's your biggest life lesson so far?

My biggest life lesson so far would be that no matter what you don't have to look to fill the void in your heart with sex, drugs, and alcohol. Always listen to the voice inside you when it says that this man is dangerous.

10. What advice would you give to your younger self or to a child in a similar position as you were when you were young?

Never be afraid to tell an adult about the abuse. Never feel like you have to be the adult in the family. Abuse and rape is never okay. That God loves you and He can heal the brokenness.

11. What does it feel like to live in prison?

To live in prison for me is like a time warp. I don't get visits or phone calls, very little mail, so I depend on God.

I treat it like another part of my street life. I adapt and blend.

12. How do you feel about the prison system or the justice system?

The justice system is not very fair. I am not a repeat offender, never been in trouble, have extenuating circumstances, should have received probation and instead received a 20 year sentence. They are harsher on women than on men and the smaller counties are harder on us as well. I believe it should be a case by case basis, not because I am female, when a man can have the same charge and walk away with less time.

The prison system, I believe, needs to work on its parole and release. They hold us so long and I don't feel like they offer enough to rehabilitate us to move back into society, especially those with large sentences.

13. What makes you laugh?

My husband and his humor and my children. I love jokes and animals.

14. Finish the sentence:
If I could change the world, I would start by bringing each person closer to God to bring peace and love and joy, one heart at a time.

I believe that God has plans for us all and he uses each of us to help others make those plans succeed.

I wish that I had found God sooner and married my current husband.

I am inspired by the promises the Bible holds for my future.

15. Please share anything else you'd like. This is your space. And your voice.

I am a God fearing Christian woman now. I trust him to restore my family to me and and take me home sooner than what TDCJ says.

Because I grew up not knowing what real love was, I lived a life that was very dangerous and sad. I was a very cold-hearted, dark souled person. I filled that void with men. I became a sex addict. A very sad life. For years, the best part of my life was my two girls. That was the only reason I lived. I have tried to commit suicide so many times; it's very scary. I felt like I was worthless and an unfit mother, that my children would be better off without me, that the world would be better off without me. I am here to tell you that is never true. Even if you feel all alone, there is always someone who loves you and wants you around.

I would love to share my whole testimony if you are interested.

Lacey Williams

July 5, 2018

Lacey,

I will begin at the end: I am so grateful you are here. Just by you choosing to write to me, I feel humbled and more aware. I feel touched that you shared. And I feel certain that the world is fuller because you are here.

I say I feel humbled because I am amazed at the abuse you have had to carry and I feel utterly unqualified to offer you anything but my ears and my love. If you have more testimony to share and you feel safe sharing it with me, I promise to listen and simply to love you through it.

Having said that, know that the pain you have endured does not define you to me. What defines you to me is the way you talk about love, especially loving yourself. "I have learned to love everything about me," you wrote. You are powerful. What I also see in you is awareness and vital lessons that will pass through your spirit and on to others you touch, including your children. You may not see them, but I trust that they feel you and carry you with them.

Your letter touched my heart and also left me feeling angry: "I don't get visits or phone calls, very little mail," you wrote. "So I depend on God." I am angry because you are right: how are you expected to heal during this long confinement without nourishing support, without opportunities to grow, learn, transform—"rehabilitation," as you called it. Friendship is healing. Connection is healing. Touch is healing. Being in community is healing. Isolation is a weak excuse for rehabilitation.

We all depend on each other's wellness. So not only do you deserve better, but we all do. We should all root for you to get the resources and fulfillment prisons so scarcely provide.

Which brings me to your husband, who seems to nourish you with his laughter and his relationship with our creator. Tell me more about him. When did you meet? Do you get to see him often?

Thank you, again, for reaching out to me. I would like to include your voice in my project. Anything else you'd like to share, I welcome it.

With kindness,
Ashley

July 6, 2018

Dear Ashley,

It was a breath of fresh air to read your letter. It made me feel very good to know that just a small portion of my testimony could impact someone like it did you. My heart soared with joy to hear your beautiful words. To say that you feel humbled from my letter to you touches me in a way I never thought possible. So thank you for that. I pray to God every day to enlarge my borders so that I may touch more lives for his glory and I believe this is a door he has opened for me. He has always pushed me to help others even before I knew him. Let me share my testimony with you and you can share with me the Glory I give to Jesus.

So I will start with my father leaving us at a very young age. My first dose of feeling abandonment. My mother moved around and moved men in and out. We lived with men in crummy trailer parks and other places. We moved in with a man who was an alcoholic and my mom worked all day. She left us with this man. He molested me at age four and physically abused me and my sister. My mother came home one day and found us locked in the closet and took us away in the middle of the night. She never knew about the sexual abuse till two years ago.

We moved a lot. We were homeless living in a tent on the Rio Grande. My mom would leave me and my sister in that tent while she went to work or did whatever she did. My mom's father helped her buy a trailer house and we had a house.

Nothing changed. She still had men come and go and the abuse to her and me never stopped. She ended up getting involved with a few men from the cartel and things got scary. She ended up being put into protective custody and she sent me and my sister to my dad's and his new wife. But before all that I had started smoking cigarettes by the age of eight and weed by the time I was ten. Got my first tattoo at age ten by a cartel member who lived next door to us.

When I was living with my dad and stepmom, they tried to buy our love. Well they succeeded with my sister. Me, though, that's not what I wanted. Things never stayed. They could be taken. So I didn't get along with them either.

I started dating, really dating, in the 5th grade, mostly Mexicans which didn't sit well with my family who is prejudiced. Then in 6th grade I started dating black boys, one which got mad at me and held me upside down off the 2nd story landing of our school. I fought all these men and boys. I had courage then, or some may say stupidity. I say it was survival mode.

It stayed that same way with different men. I started to party a lot to hide the fact that I had no real family. That's when I found my family. I became a member of a gang, selling and a little using at that time.

Then when I was 15, I was raped again, which devastated me. I tried to tell my family and nobody believed me. So that is when I really spiraled. I moved back with my mom and really started partying. I was sleeping with pretty much any man. I started dating a college guy named Christopher and he was great in the beginning. Then, at parties, he would let anyone have sex with me. I let it happen. I didn't think I was worth much more than that.

I drank 24/7 and started using cocaine. By the time I was 16 I could down two big bottles of Jack Daniels straight. I had started fighting all the time, getting kicked outta school, so my mom told me she couldn't handle me so she sent me back to my dad's. So I had to face the guy that raped me everyday at school. I had a hard time handling that. This is when I met my now husband Kevin Williams. My best friend.

I really dove into the cocaine. It numbed the pain the most and I could move a lot of drugs for my people. My husband is a black man. I fell in love with him. I was just so scared to say anything to him, I was afraid he didn't feel the same way and I would lose my best friend. Turns out he felt the same way.

Now during all this time I had tried to commit suicide at least a dozen times. My first attempt was when I was about 12 years old. The last time was November 2016 sitting in county jail.

I ended up getting pregnant with my drug dealer's baby. Then he left to get clean. I met one of his best friends. My dad and stepmom fell in love with him (my ex-husband Roy). So then I lost the baby. Roy and I were still doing cocaine together. Then I realized he was my ticket out of the house. My parents saved up for my sister to go to college, but not me, never even asked if I wanted to go. So the white man that they loved was my ticket out. So he asked me to marry him and, knowing my plan to use him to get out of my house, I said yes. He was or is an alcoholic but not really any abuse at the time.

I got pregnant. I graduated high school May 2000, married June 2000, had my oldest daughter Ashley October 2000. She was very sick so we spent lots of time in the hospital. After Roy and I got married, the emotional and mental abuse started about a week later. I was married to Roy for 15 years and the abuse just got worse. He had me convinced I could do no better than him.

I had my youngest daughter Kody November 2004. In 2010 I started going to nursing school. I had found a decent job and was getting my confidence back and was trying to make the marriage work till I got out of nursing school. My youngest daughter Kody told me one night after a big fight, "Momma, Dad should not push you against the wall like that." That was my wake up call that I was teaching my girls that it was ok to be with an abusive man. My oldest, Ashley, had helped me clean up after many fights. It's not right. I was putting my children through the same thing my mom had put me through. So I kicked him out and then the summer rolled around and the girls went to stay with family for the summer.

Roy started fights all the time thinking he still had control of me. Still. But with the girls gone, I couldn't stand the alone, the quiet. Too many demons and skeletons making noise, so I turned back to drugs and alcohol and men again. Do you see a pattern here? I do now. I was trying to fill a big void in my heart. I needed true love. So the end of summer rolled around. The girls came home and, well, I was a functioning drunk and drug user again. I went out every night to the bars to find a man to sleep with. So then the house we were living in I couldn't pay the mortgage so it was foreclosed and we moved around. Then I found someone to rent me a two bedroom one bath, but it was me and the girls. I was trying to clean up again and get my life straight. I was struggling to find a job, a legal job. I was trying not to start selling again.

So then I met this man Brian on the Internet. He painted a beautiful picture of a perfect life and I fell for it, hook line and sinker. I fell in love with him. He turned out to be the worst man I had been with.

Then things got rocky and we broke up. I met another man named Josh and I know that God put him and his family in my life to try and save me from this. But I screwed that up because, well, all the positive love he gave me scared me and I cheated on him, and I ran straight back to Brian because it was negative and normal. That's when things got really bad.

He made me sleep with other men and video it and if I did something wrong I got beat. Then he started to push me to pick up a woman, which I had or have no interest in. It's like Hell's Gates were wide open now. The beatings got so bad and the threats that by the time I saw what was going on, it was too late to run.

So one night my oldest wanted to do some drinking. I was unsure about that but Brian talked me into it and into letting a couple of her friends join. They drank, I had a few drinks and smoked some weed. I was not right in the head. He had full control over me. So here is how I ended up in prison. This is where most people want to judge, but I know who I am in God's eyes.

So one of the females at the house, not my daughter but one of her friends, she tried to kiss me several times. I had been arguing with Brian all night. Well he was on the phone when this girl kissed me and I pushed her away and told her no, I don't want no part of that. Well like I said he had been wanting me to be with a female. So then the fighting really started and I told him no. He told me that if I did not do what he wanted, he would finish me off and do whatever he wanted to do with my girls especially Ashley. So I went into protection mode for my girls. My thought was well she wanted it and I am saving my girls. So then I was forced to leave the house after I had sexual relations with this girl. I got beat cause it was not up to his standards.

The next day my oldest sent a text that they had gotten all their stuff and were staying with their uncle. I drove back to town and found out that I was being charged with rape of an underage girl. I lost my children and started to spiral again. I called Brian and he said that he was gonna help me. His way of helping was forcing me into prostitution. He worked me from Texas, New Mexico, Arizona, Colorado, California. I definitely started using drugs again, and I was beat on a regular basis. I had at least 4 major concussions within a year and a half. Two almost cost me my life. I have nerve damage down the left side of my body and face. I lost some hearing.

So I am in prison for Agg. Sexual Assault/Child. Brian was never found. Texas Rangers said he was a ghost. It took me six months to tell the lawyer about all that Brian had done. I was so scared of him. I thought that he could get to me in jail, too.

So I was locked up on April 19, 2016. One of my real good friends, actually he is family for real now, got me to open the bible and read Matthew 6:25-34. Now God placed several different people in my life to help me grow closer to him and understand his word.

I have no family at this point. My family has disowned me for two reasons. I am with a black man and my crime. This is when God brought me Kevin and told me that he was the husband I had been asking for all this time, and Kevin said God brought him to me. He told me he would never lose me ever again. He looked for me for a while after I was taken away.

So during all this time I had started building a relationship with God. God had told me to sign for the 20 years and he got me to trust him and I would not do all my time. So I trusted him and here I am. Right before Kevin came into my life again I had tried to commit suicide again. I was diagnosed with depression, multiple personality disorder, and a form of PTSD called Battered Woman Syndrome. That's when I started getting my meds and finally I was numb again and it was great. Then Kevin came into my life and God forced me to fall for him. Well I already loved him, I just had to feel. He is a very positive man, God fearing. He is full of so much love. I know that if I had not been locked up I would've ran away from his positive love also but God. I came to prison May 16, 2017, I was baptized August 2017 and I am in the faith-based dorm all of which I never asked to do or be a part of. But God. I was able to take a business computer class and graduate. Other women have been turned down for the reasons of their crime, same crime as mine. But God. God has given me several dreams since being in the faith-based dorm. The latest was that I got a program. So I wrote a letter to the Board of the program and they are sending my request to the placement specialist. This is a pre-release program so I would be released on parole after completion of the program. The thing is I am here for a 20 year sentence and per mandate (TDCJ) I have to do half. I have only a year and some change done. But God. I know that God has been waiting to take me off this detour. Waiting on me to fully release my anger, guilt, shame, resentment. I have finally leaned in completely to God and given him all my trust. God has definitely taught me to love myself. That was a big problem. I could look in the mirror and never really look at myself. I hated what I saw. I had for years. I do love everything about me, the things that used to make me cringe I smile and know that God allowed me to go through the things I did cause he needs a soldier to touch others like me. I truly know how to love others and myself and it's the best feeling.

As I said before my family has disowned me. So I don't get mail or visits or phone calls from them. As for Kevin I get letters from him. It has been since April 2017 that I talked to him or saw him. I miss him so much. I miss his voice, his touch. He just moved to Oklahoma and is struggling to find a job. He is an ex-felon. He has a forgery charge. He moved away from the negative influences to better our futures. He has claim land on the reservation and is working on getting our house built. Money is tight. I depend on God for all my needs. Like I said no visits, phone calls, no commissary, very little mail. I wish there was a way that Kevin could get here. I am praying that God opens a door so Kevin can come to my graduation on July 28, 2018. His pickup is broke down and so he will have to rent a car for that weekend.

He is 35 and he is an amazing happy man. He always makes me smile. He brings light to my life. I have known him for 20+ years. He is my best friend. He has had a lot of trouble with women. We struggle with the same insecurities. We fit together in so many ways. He is my knight in shining armor and he takes that job very seriously. He is a great father even when he thinks he's not. He is a great provider. He loves with so much passion you can feel it in his letters and in person. I know that he wants to come see me just as bad as I want him to. God will open a door. He is my soul mate.

Wow that was really great. I have never wrote all that out. I have had people hear bits and pieces of my life and tell me I should write a book. To be honest I have thought about it. But like I tell people I wouldn't know how to start. But I guess writing it all out really makes a difference. I just recently became comfortable with my situation. I used to be afraid of telling people my crime. I am not anymore because I know that God will protect me and he gives me the strength.

I do wish that the prison system would be more willing to help transform or rehabilitate inmates. Some of us truly want to change and go home.

Please feel free to use any and all of my testimony in your project or even future projects. I look forward to building a friendship with you.

Thank you so much for listening.

Your friend,
Lacey Williams

P.S. Let me add a little about my girls. So the last time I saw Ashley she was my mini-me. She acted like me, looked like me, talked like me. She was a lover not a fighter. She loved to laugh and always had a smile on her beautiful face. She was always making crazy faces. My favorite things I miss and love about Ashley is her Love. She was never shy about showing her affection toward me in public. At home she was always snuggling up with me whether it was in bed early in the morning or in the recliner watching a movie. She was always right by my side. Actually she was always on my right side. I miss hearing, "Mom, I love you." I miss seeing her smile at me.

So now my little fireball Kody. She was my spit fire, she was my fighter. She didn't like to be held for long periods of time. She always stuck up for Ashley. She is four years younger and was fighting Ashley's battles. She was fearless. She started kindergarten in a cast and her fearlessness just intensified with age. I loved that about her but Lord knows it made me worry about her so much. She kept me on my toes, but you know she always watched out for me too. She always took care of me and her sister. Sad really that an 11 year old felt like she had to take care of her 30 year old mother. Now I understand why she started developing ulcers by the time she was 10. What a mother I was.

You know I miss her craziness. And I would say that my favorite thing I miss the most from her is when she would wrap her arms and legs around my neck and squeeze so hard. She would wrap her legs around me and hang on like a monkey. I miss the little smile when she would slide in next to Ashley and I and cuddle. Always on the left side.

I miss how when we were all together how much fun we had and how we all laughed. I am very thankful that my children have stayed together and close through this.

So God had been showing me after I got to prison that Kody would be the first to want to see me. Well on my way to prison the officers who brought me said she had pushed and bugged everyone until they approved a visit with my girls. Ashley couldn't decide if she wanted to see me. But Kody did.

I caught chain before I had a chance to see them or even say bye to Kevin. God has a plan I am sure. I know that God will restore them to me soon.

I thank you so much for listening to me.

Lacey

July 15, 2018

Lacey,

I read through your letter more than once, although even the first time it hung heavy and spoke loudly. And the word that's coming to mind now is "proud"—proud that you had the courage and guts and confidence in who you are to share your testimony, and I'm honored that you trusted me with it. That you trusted me to carry your story forward and, together, enlarge our borders.

I feel compelled to put your full testimony in the book. And I think one of the reasons why is because people like me may not know that people with testimonies like yours exist everyday in this country. That when we talk about progress or policy or poverty or equality or social justice in this country, we must remember that we have left too many behind—and that we continue to do so. And this is not ok.

This may sound naive, but I didn't fully imagine that little girls grow up in this country with stories like yours. And that, I am sure, you are not the only one. That little girls grow up in tents and start smoking cigarettes by age eight. So seamlessly have we (those in power) written over stories and lives like yours that, to someone like me, it is very easy not to hear about lives like yours. Not to know or imagine they exist. Not to know that public policy is failing you. Not to know that the prison system is an impoverished and wholly inadequate response to your experience and that it, too, is failing you. Which means that it is failing all of us.

But you are upending this because you are not afraid to speak out. With your voice, you are adding to the wave of change. It begins here, with voices no longer silenced, forcibly or out of fear. You are bold and you are needed. Purpose, indeed.

I believe your life path has, ultimately, led you to discover this about yourself, the hard way, but I want to reiterate just in case: you are worthy of love. Healthy love. Love that is gentle and kind and present and honoring. Self-love.

You deserve a place on this planet and you are here for a reason. Live your purpose.

Within you is a daring voice that deserves to say "yes" and "no" when it wants. And it is powerful.

Your friend,
Ashley

Robert

Seven.

June 15, 2018

Hi Ashley,

I think it is amazing what you are doing, pulling together stories of inmates to show that we are for the most decent human beings.
A lot of us have interesting stories to tell, but very few people are willing to listen.

1. So, a little about myself. I was born in Texas, but grew up in Oklahoma. My birth mom gave me up for adoption, but I was not adopted until I was 9. I spent 6 years in foster care. I was a seriously messed up kid, and my adopted parents did not know what to do with me, so they put me in a children's home. I stayed there, only going home for holidays, until I graduated High School. I graduated as a junior, then went into the Navy. That did not turn out well. I loved my time in the Navy, but my mind and heart were full of problems. Have been all my life.
I never really had a stable life or home, even though that is all I really wanted.

There are more details than this, I just wanted to give you an overview. I look forward to answering the rest of your questions, and communicating with you.

This was just to touch base and ensure you that I am very interested in participating in your project.

Sincerely,
Robert

June 18, 2018

Robert,

Thank you for your prompt reply and, most sincerely, for being willing to share your story and your voice. I am grateful for your trust in me and in this project. I promise to treat you and your story with respect, which is, of course, what you deserve.

Know that I am thinking of you, rooting for you, and eagerly awaiting the chance to hear more of who you are.

With gratitude,
Ashley

June 29, 2018

Hey Ashley,

Sorry that it took so long to write back. We were on lockdown this past week. This is done every quarter so they can shake us down for contraband, weapons, and drugs. Anyways, here is some more input on the questions you asked. I was open and honest, despite my worry about what you might think about what I had to say.

2. What I look like:
Well, quite frankly I look a little rough. I used to be in pretty good shape when I was in the Navy. But then I discovered I love being a chef, and started working in restaurants. I got big real fast. I was almost 270 lbs when I was arrested in 2009. I have lost some weight since then, but I admittedly am still out of shape. I really need to work out more.
My hair is brown (and a little grey), and my eyes are hazel. The eyes are my favorite part of my looks because they actually change color. They go from green to brown around the edges. What's kind of weird is that when I was younger, my eyes were dark brown and my hair was VERY blonde.

I actually have 2 tattoos, a tiger on my shoulder, and a dreamcatcher on my back. The tiger was actually my 19th birthday present. Some guys from my command wanted to get tats, so I drove. They picked the tat and paid for it before I even knew what happened. I was totally freaked out because I was terrified of needles for a long time. (Messed up story for another time.) I went through with it though.

The dreamcatcher was designed by a friend of mine, and it turned out pretty awesome.

3. My family:
I was adopted. My birth mom was 17 when I was born, and I have 2 biological brothers. She put us in foster care when I was still very little, but I was not adopted until the age of 9. Both of my brothers were adopted almost immediately by the families that fostered them. I went through multiple families in a few years, some were actually good, a couple were abusive (emotionally, physically, and/or sexually). I was actually adopted by the same family that adopted my oldest little brother. You would think that was a good thing, but not so much. Admittedly, part of it was my fault because of my emotional and behavior problems, and the fact that I became sexually aware and active at a very young age. Part of it was them too, they did not know how to deal with me, and did not have the patience to do so when they had other younger children to attend to. My parents adopted 6 children overall, 4 girls, and me and my brother.

A mere 3 years after I was adopted, I was put in a children's home. I got to go home for holidays and summer vacation. They tried to make me a part of the family, but I had so much anger and psychological problems I pretty much stayed an outsider.

It wasn't until years later did I finally build a rapport with them. My mom even offered for me to move back to Texas and help me have a fresh start. I said no because I had built a life here in Virginia. That was a huge mistake on my part. Had I taken my family up on that offer, I probably would not be in prison.

No one in my family has spoken to me since I got locked up. That was nine years ago. My oldest little sister called one time trying to get a hold of me, but I have not heard from her since.

4. Children
I don't have any children of my own. I had the opportunity to be a father on several occasions, but they were either taken from me, or I blew it myself. I dated the same woman off and on for several years, she had 2 abortions and a miscarriage. My ex wife had stillborn twins. One girlfriend had a baby, but there was no guarantee that it was mine.
I was going to adopt my fiancee's daughter when we got married, but I committed my crime.

There is pretty much no chance I will ever have a family of my own. I've had multiple chances, but blew them. Now, with my crime, and the time I face, it would take a miracle. I believe in miracles, as I believe in God and Jesus with all my heart, so who knows.

5. Goals
There are a couple of dreams that I have, but I have no idea how to accomplish them. My first main goal is to tell my story about my life and my crime. I am a sex offender, and there were multiple warning signs when I was younger that were ignored. I want the chance to share how and why I ended up the way I did, the things that I went through that put me in the mindset to commit such a crime. PLEASE keep in mind that I am not making excuses. I confessed my crime. I simply hope that I can help others see the same warning signs that were ignored in my life, to possibly save them from traveling the same road I did, keeping other underage children safe. There

are few, if any, people in my position that are willing to give an inside view of these types of crimes.

My second main goal is much more mundane and less painful or disturbing. I want to launch a line of Christian inspirational products called Gospel Gear. I have the company logo and several product ideas already, but I do not know how to trademark any of it, nor do I have the money.

I also have a really good idea for a restaurant that is specifically designed around diabetic diets. Many restaurants have a few items for diabetics, but those people usually have to make real sacrifices to eat out. A menu built around diabetics would be good, healthy food for everyone, without being so limited and restricted.

6. Leave prison for a day.
If I could leave prison for a day, I would reach out to the people I hurt so I could ask for forgiveness for what I did.
I think I'd eat at Golden Corral so I could enjoy all the different food I've been missing. A movie would be pretty cool too.

I hope this info was useful and enlightening. If you have any questions or want me to expand on anything I have said, please let me know.

Sincerely,
Robert

July 7, 2018

Robert,

I want to thank you for speaking your truth. It takes courage to share so openly, especially with a stranger like me. Know that I am grateful for your trust in me and I will do my best to honor you and your story.

If I know anything, it is that I am not here to judge you. I am here to listen and acknowledge your truth.

For a moment, I wondered if I am wrong. I am involved with an organization called Exhale to Inhale, which supports survivors of domestic and sexual violence to find peace and safety in their bodies and lives, again, through the grounding and healing practice of yoga. And, so, I wondered, should I not be so understanding with you? Is it counterintuitive to support survivors and also have a desire to see and care about you? I'm laughing to myself just imagining that thought now: of course it's not counterintuitive. Supporting survivors does not exclude supporting those who have made mistakes (and, after all, you're a survivor, too). If anything, it calls for supporting both even more. We all need healing. We all deserve love. Nothing will change if we deny anyone love. That is not the answer.

When I received your letter a few days ago and, at the top, you wrote that you were "open and honest, despite my worry about what you might think," it hung heavy on my heart. I don't want you to have to carry worry about what I might think. I want you to feel at ease to express who you are with me because I would want the same in return.

I published a book called *The Moon and Her Sisters* in April, and in it I had written this:

I am not ruined
by my expectations of myself.
I am ruined by what I've imagined
are yours.

I just wanted to share that with you.

The other thing I'm thinking about is how you described your adoptive parents: "they did not know how to deal with me." I understand both sides, how they must have felt, too, but I also think about how that must have made you feel as a child: without safety. As children, these little beings with brains still developing as we're navigating the world, we must feel out of control often. And, so, what we have to rely upon for our sense of safety is the adults in our lives who remind us and show us they are there to protect us, that they have any bump in the road that comes our way covered. I can't imagine what's it's like to be without that support and to experience so much upheaval in your young life.

Which brings me here, to the dreamcatcher tattooed on your back. Hearing that you had chosen a dreamcatcher to anoint your body immediately drew me in. I believe they were meant, traditionally, to protect children while they slept and, of course, to catch dreams. So, tell me, why did you choose the dreamcatcher and what dreams do you hope to catch?

In friendship,
Ashley

July 18, 2018

Ashley,

The fact that you won't judge me, and are still willing to listen to what I have to say, speaks much for your heart and character. I have been surprised over the years at not being judged and condemned like I thought I would. There have been some rough times, and some harsh people, but by and large, people have accepted me for who I am, not what I did.

As for the dreamcatcher, I am part Native American. I was studying Indian and Wiccan beliefs for a while, and decided to receive a dreamcatcher to protect me from my nightmares. I used to have chronic nightmares when I was younger, some so bad that they were night terrors. I would wake up friends, family and girlfriends from deep sleep because of them. I would even sleepwalk at times. I actually almost got kicked out of boot camp (I was in the Navy) because of it.

As for my childhood, I absolutely never felt safe or secure. I was even put in a mental institution at one point, and there were all kinds of problems there. I never truly received the help or understanding that I needed, especially when I tried to tell adults that I had been abused. I was ignored, not believed, or they minimized what I told them. I had serious self confidence issues, and was very socially inept due to my own unstable environment. Besides mental, emotional, and sexual abuse, I was introduced to actual sex at a very young age.

To be honest, that is why I hate what I did even more. I manipulated and took advantage of an underage girl, just like I was manipulated. I saw the warning signs, and similarities, but did not heed them.

I wanted to answer more questions in this email, but I have been long winded enough as it is. I look forward to your response and answering more of your questions. (It is very hard to type on this little keyboard on my media player, and autocorrect sucks.)

Sincerely,
Robert

July 30, 2018

Ashley,

I have been meditating on your next couple of questions, and these are my thoughts.

7. Purpose/Mission

I absolutely believe that each person has a purpose in life, but not everyone fulfills it or lives up to their potential. As contrary as it seems, sometimes a person has to fall and be broken before they discover their true strength and purpose. I did something unforgivable and lost everything and everyone, but I am now a completely different person. I am stronger, wiser, and see the world around me with new eyes.

My mission and purpose is to be an example of forgiveness and redemption, and a warning to those who would ignore/dismiss depression and statements of abuse. I also wish to share my faith as a Christian, demonstrating what my faith has done for me and how it changed me.

Too many children, and adults, have their problems minimized or blown off completely by those who are supposed to care for them, and that is what needs to change in order to stop the cycle of abuse.

8. A Good Friend

What makes a good friend? Well my answer to that has definitely changed over the years, for the better I might add. I was, for the most part, not a very good friend when I was younger. I used and manipulated pretty much everyone around me, not really trusting anyone. I know

now that this came from me hating myself and not facing the pain from my past. If you cannot like and trust yourself first, you will never be able to truly be close to anyone.

A true friend is someone who will be there for you when you need them, build you up instead of tearing you down. It is someone you can trust, someone you can be honest with, someone who is dependable. My absolute best friend is Daniel, a man that has had my back and been there for me no matter what I was going through. Even 9 years into prison, he has still been there for me.

9. Biggest Life Lesson

This question had me stumped for a while, but I have learned quite a bit in the past several years. Problems and fears cannot be overcome by hiding and running from them. Doing so only makes things worse, becoming harder to resolve the longer those problems and fears fester.

Don't hold onto anger and bitterness. They will take root and spread, infecting every part of your life. Have you ever seen a wall that has been covered in vines for a long time? Or a tree growing close to a sidewalk? The roots separate and tear apart the very foundation of the building and ground. That is unchecked bitterness. I hated myself for so long, allowing the bullying and negativity aimed at me to shape who I was. No more. I no longer allow what others think of me to hold me back, not even the condemnation from my crime. I know who I am, what I am about, where my unshakable faith is.

I would like to share with you my current biggest fear. I am afraid of having to serve all 30 years of my sentence.

Do not get it wrong, I deserve the time I got and I accept that. But I would be 59 years old upon release with no one to be there for me and no where to go. Even if I was released sooner, I am still honestly afraid that I will never again have a chance to have a family.

I have rambled enough already. I do not know if what I am sharing is helping you or even what you are looking for, but I am exceedingly glad to talk to you. You make it incredibly easy. I look forward to hearing from you soon.

Sincerely,
Robert

Deidre

Eight.

June 30, 2018

1. Introduce yourself! Tell me a little about you:

I am a writer! I write for *The Echo,* a Texas prisoner's newspaper that is distributed to 148,000 inmates. I hold two positions on the paper: Unit Reporter and Contributing Writer. Enclosed herewith is also my book, *Freedom — A Daily Devotional.*

I love to exercise because I believe it's a natural remedy to physical and psychological ailments. I'm very into health and wellbeing.

I try to see everyone's perspective in conflicts. I am a Christian but not as fundamentally charged as the bible commands. To emphasize what I mean, I can give you an example: I am a lesbian and today I'm okay with that decision. I fought it for a long time because of the way I was raised to believe it was wrong. Plus, I never loved any man. I had sexual relations with some, hence my children, but never close to the connection I feel with another woman.

I got my paralegal diploma since I've been in here, plus some college. I love to run and play basketball.

2. Describe what you look like. What do you like about how you look? Is there something you wish you could change?

Well, there is a picture on the back of my book, but I can say that I have dark, curly hair. I am 9 years older than that photo, but look pretty much the same. What I like about my looks is that they reflect my personality and character. My looks spell warmth, compassion, and invitation.

At times, I wish I could cause people to see past my beauty. But not all the time. Who doesn't want to be beautiful? But what I mean by this is that it can deflect one's attention from seeing, or wanting to see, what's inside me, which is more valuable. I've grown weary of men looking at me like I'm a piece of meat and men taking advantage of me as a child. In retrospect, Beauty has power. In the past, I have used my beauty and charm to my advantage. Once I used it to get a job in an area I had no experience. The guy thought I was cute and wanted to look at me all day so I just stood around and earned good money doing little to nothing.

3. Do you have family? If so, tell me about them.

My mom and I have more of a friendship. We used drugs together and I have spent 9 years of my life in prison while she was out there using. I educated myself and now it's like she is the child and I'm the mother. She looks up to me and I am very protective of her. She's actually in prison, too, and gets out in October. Until yesterday, she was on this unit with me. But they transferred her. My father was never there for me. Period. But since I have been in prison this time, a lawyer in his 70s has befriended me and now I think of him as my godfather. He does a lot for me and I love him very much. I consider my close friends family, too. I have made some good ones in here. I have 4 brothers and sisters on my mom's side. We were raised by her primarily with a few stepdads along the way. We all have different fathers. My perception of a father was distorted as a child because of sexual abuse.

4. Do you have children? If so, what do you most love about them? What do you miss about them?

I have three children. My oldest is 14 and she is the only one I have a "sort of" relationship with. Her father gained custody when she was 6 months old and I have been in and out of her life in between prison sentences. There's definitely some repair work to do. The other two —a son, 8 years old, and a daughter, 12 years old—were adopted by my second cousins when they were infants. I did what was best for them at the time, which was giving them up. But as far as my oldest, I love the fact that she is smart, innovative, and an entrepreneur. So is the youngest daughter from what I hear.

I miss what I don't know about them. I guess the more appropriate term would be, "I long for."

5. What are your goals?

My goal is to be a successful writer. Not for the fame but for the feeling of accomplishment and fulfillment of purpose. That means being able to help, love, and inspire others to find and express themselves freely.

6. If you could leave prison for a day, what would you do?

Visit family. Eat well. Take photos.

7. Do you believe your life has a purpose or specific mission? What is it?

To write. And to help others as a servant in any way I can that will enable them to be their best self, learning from my experiences. Life is too short to learn EVERYTHING from trial and error so we must be able to learn from the mistakes of others. And Lord knows I have made enough of them.

8. What do you think makes a good friend?

Empathy, attention, willingness, and the ability to see everyone's perspective. Or consider it, rather.

9. What's your biggest life lesson so far?

That there is good in everyone—even those who have committed the most heinous crimes. People just need someone to help them manifest their goodness. Everyone deserves the benefit of doubt and love, despite their attitudes.

Leading by example is the only way to make people more positive. I was shown a different way to live and be through paying attention to the actions of others.

I've also learned not to allow my expectations to rule me.

10. What advice would you give to your younger self or to a child in a similar position as you were when you were young?

Forgive everyone everything. And before you do something that might harm someone, physically, mentally, or emotionally, put yourself in their shoes and see how it would feel if it were done to you first.

11. What does it feel like to live in prison?

Oppressive.

The officers make it hard. Inmates, too. But you can always tell what kind of day it's going to be by who the officer that comes on shift to work in your dorm is going to be. It ebbs and flows, really. Even prisoners have good days that are filled with laughter and fun. Mine do, anyway.

The inmates make it hard, too. They argue and focus on each other's faults. My frustration comes from witnessing these encounters and trying to figure out how to effectively communicate with them.

12. How do you feel about the prison system or the justice system?

The prison system is corrupt and secretive. Stuff goes on where we have no defense because it's us against the officers and staff and, as inmates, we are never right. If it's our word against theirs, they believe them every time. Plus, they pick at us about shit that in no way will contribute to our rehabilitation. Like leaving a pencil on the table while you aren't in your cubicle!?! For that you can get written up and given 30 days no rec, 30 days no commissary, and 30 days cell restriction. Oh, and they can take all your property for 30 days. Nothing to do. Not even a book. If you get caught with one during that period, you can get an additional 30 days of all of the above. How is that for rehabilitation?

On the subject of rehabilitation, in the state of Texas, if you come to prison for a drug crime, they won't even begin to consider you for treatment (besides one A.A. meeting a week) until you become eligible for parole and the board votes you into the program. By that time, you have already been locked up for years. So there isn't much offered in the way of addressing the issues that brought us here. You have to learn on your own and not everyone has that capability.

As far as the justice system, in Texas anyway, the sentences are way unfair. My neighbor in here got 5 years for manslaughter. I got 30 years for possessing one counterfeit hundred dollar bill. That's just one example. I don't think that the range of punishment/sentences should be so widely left open to human judgment. Because, you know, if you get charged with a felony in a small county, you are going to get the maximum, and if you get charged in a big county, it's like a mill. They shuffle you through with small sentences. I feel like the justice system is a way for counties to make money also. They put you on probation with all these fees.

In retrospect, I don't believe there should be no punishment for crimes. Our country needs justice for people who are wronged by people who are doing wrong. But the wrongdoers are still human and they need help in learning to do right, not thrown away in a place where they learn even more bad behaviors in prison or get bitter from doing all the time in such an oppressive place.

13. What makes you laugh?

I laugh when I hear others laughing. When people are being silly. It's contagious, you know.

14. Finish the sentence:
If I could change the world, I would reveal to
everyone their full potential and remove selfishness and
greed.

I believe that love has no bounds and doesn't
discriminate. The past is my lesson, the present is a gift,
and the future is my motivation.

I wish the world would see through God's eyes.

I am inspired by writing and reading what others write.

15. Please share anything else you'd like. This is your
space. And your voice.

*below are excerpts from Deidre's book *Freedom — A
Daily Devotional*

When I first saw him juggle and make a coin disappear,
my 9-year-old mind was intrigued. He was a magician for
children's parties and lived in our trailer park. He asked
my mom if he could teach me some tricks. Over the next
few years he taught me more than that. He taught me
about sex during my "internship" as a magician. He even
molested my little brother and had a baby with my mom
(my little sister). Almost 15 years later I have forgiven him
as he sits in a Huntsville prison, while I, having been
shaped by my abusive past and poor choices afterwards,
sit in a Gatesville prison. Today I take responsibility for
my choices because I am an adult and refuse to be the
victim anymore. I can't keep letting that experience bring
me down. Instead, I make the conscious choice to be
grateful that God allowed me to make it through the
hardship, because now I can empathize with others who

have been through the same thing. Yesterday I juggled basketballs on the rec yard and made a bottle cap disappear and re-appear for some inmates. Magic tricks give them a moment of escape from the walls, and a chance to enjoy some childish delight—something some of them never get to have. Nothing that happens in your life is insignificant. God uses all of it to mold you for your ministry to others.

*

In 2004, before I went to do state jail time, I had a 2-month-old baby girl. My mother (who at the time had my 6-year-old sister and 11-year-old brother) and I were not living right. Those kids definitely deserved better. An encounter with the law caused C.P.S. to intervene in our lives. As the C.P.S. people pulled up next to our house to pick up the kids, so did another car. The other car was my third cousin's, who only a few years ago was involved in drugs and was living a crazy life similar to the way my mom and I were living at the time. Since then, he'd changed his life, now obeyed God's commands, and was headed for seminary school. He also married a Christian lady. By the grace of God, and many complications, they had one baby, but were unable to conceive again. C.P.S. ended up allowing my cousin and his wife to take the three children temporarily. After many months and much heartache (but the right choice according to God's will), they adopted all three of them. Four years later, they adopted my newborn son. I believe in God's divine intervention. It wasn't a coincidence that they pulled up after we hadn't seen them for such a long time. The Lord promises to bless those who obey Him. Since changing his life to follow the Lord, God gave him the desires of his heart…children…times four! For everyone, that was truly a blessing.

*

When I didn't get any mail (again) I was upset. I went from 2-3 letters a day to less than that in an entire week. As my neighbor listened to me complain, she said, "Well, I've been here 17 years and my family and friends fell off a long time ago." That did not help my situation or the way I was feeling…Feeling abandoned in prison is an ugly feeling and sometimes it's hard to shake off. This just proves that nothing is in our control, not even close relationships. It's not like we can pick up the phone and call our people. But, there is God and He is always pursuing us and trying to get our attention. If you feel lonely, it doesn't always mean you're "alone." If you sincerely look to God, you will find Him.

July 14, 2018

Hello Ashley,

I have so much planning to do. I made parole and will be released around November. I have absolutely NOTHING out there. I'm going to a halfway house and hope that they will provide me with some type of voucher or something to get some clothes. Texas parole only gives you $50 when you are released so that's not much. And then they expect you to pay your first month's parole fees of $18 with it! At least I'll have three pairs of panties and bras when I get out. Plus, I have a distant aunt who may be willing to help me as well. She lives in Washington, though. It's really scary. Thinking about getting out and all you have to face. I'll be ok.

I've always been a survivor, but this time I'm going to thrive. I have learned so much in the past five years about how to succeed. I've educated myself and wrote books! I have two novels that I wrote also that I want to get published. Well, I'm almost done with the second one which is a sequel to the first.

You are the type of people I want in my life, so I truly hope to have a lasting friendship with you.

Well this is all for now. Write back soon.

Deidre McDonald

Mike

Nine.

Mike's been in prison since age 16:

"I've never had sex. What I have had are a number of first-time experiences tainted by prison. I learned to shave from a crack-dealer in county jail; my boss in Patuxent's (the prison's) ID Room taught me how to tie a tie; my first roommate was a cellmate; my first and only kiss was in the visiting room at Patuxent, from Danielle, the sister of a co-worker from my brief stint at Pizza Hut.

"Frankly, I am tired of having first-time experiences dimmed by failed, unhealthy circumstances."

Martin

Ten.

April 23, 2018

1. Introduce yourself! Tell me a little about you:

Ny name is Martin Lockett and I am 39 years old. I have been incarcerated in Oregon for 14 ½ years on a 17 ½ year sentence for DUI manslaughter where I tragically killed two people and severely injured another on New Year's Eve of 2003.

While incarcerated, I have devoted my time to becoming an alcohol and drug abuse counselor as a way to bring purpose to my life and honor my victims who, ironically, were also in recovery at the time I claimed their lives. In this effort I have earned a BS in Sociology and an MS in Psychology, as well as have become a certified recovery mentor. I work in this capacity for a treatment program, accruing practicum hours toward my certification as a drug and alcohol counselor.

I have published two books (memoir and blog collection) and enjoy blogging about life—particularly my experiences in prison. I believe we all have a voice and an inherent right to be heard.

2. Describe what you look like. What do you like about how you look? Is there something you wish you could change?

I am 6 ft tall, 220 pounds, muscular frame. My favorite aspect of my physicality is my height. Life can be made more difficult for short men. If I could change one thing about how I look, it would likely be my oily skin. It can be a struggle to keep acne away, but thank goodness for the few anti-acne products the prison sells.

3. Do you have family? If so, tell me about them.

I have a twin (fraternal) brother whom I am extremely close with. He has been by my side through my entire sentence (and, sadly, the previous one where I spent over three years behind bars), supporting me in every way possible. I also have an older sister of two years, a deceased sister, two nieces, and one nephew.

My family is everything to me and I couldn't ask for more support from them through this most difficult time. In addition to having an amazing family, I have a fiancée who has unwaveringly been by my side for the past 13 years! She has supported me in all my goals and achievements along the way. She is my rock, my comfort, and my soulmate.

4. Do you have children? If so, what do you most love about them? What do you miss about them?

I do not have any children, although I did have a son who tragically passed away three weeks prior to his first birthday. He had gotten sick with the flu and it rapidly progressed into encephalitis (fluid on the brain), causing him to have a seizure that ultimately took his life.

5. What are your goals?

My main goal coming into this prison sentence was to become a certified alcohol and drug counselor. I have already met most of my educational goals by attaining my master's in psychology, but I have decided I am going to pursue a Ph.D in clinical psychology when I am released. This will be a 5-year endeavor, and when I complete it I will apply for a license to practice psychology.

I will, in the meantime, work as a substance abuse counselor, mentor, and public speaker. I will be involved with DUI victim impact panels in my community where I tell my story of the dangers of drinking and driving. I will also look to speak at schools, colleges, jails and prisons, telling my story of poor decision-making, consequences, and turning insurmountable odds into purpose, meaning, and victory.

I plan to write one or two more post-prison books, create a successful blog site, and eventually open my own psychology practice that specializes in substance addiction treatment. This will happen within 10 years of being released from prison in 2021.

6. If you could leave prison for a day, what would you do?

If I could leave prison for a day, I would spend the day at my brother's house with my family and fiancée (no friends). I would want to eat a nice meal with them, talk with them, and get away for more private time with my fiancée. We would do a lot of hugging, some laughing, and likely a little crying toward the end of our day. But these precious moments and memories would carry me through the remaining three years of my long sentence.

7. Do you believe your life has a purpose or specific mission? What is it?

When this happened over 14 years ago, I felt that my life mattered not. I was deep in my addiction and lived with a huge void. Nothing mattered beyond getting drunk and having wild, reckless "fun." In the aftermath of this tragedy, I discovered my victims were in recovery at the time of their deaths. They had devoted their lives to helping others get clean and sober and were beloved in their community—my community. When I learned of their lives and work via *The Oregonian*, I made it my life's mission to honor them by carrying on their legacies and doing all I could to help others through their addiction. This is what spurred my drive to become a substance abuse counselor.

In addition to helping mentor others through their treatment and recovery efforts, I also co-facilitate the impaired driver victim impact panels. Here, I am able to tell my story and use the pain of this tragedy to effect change in others, spread awareness, and help others begin to heal from their own pain. It is truly rewarding to be a part of others' change process in multiple ways; this gives my life purpose and meaning. This makes my work not feel like work, and the fulfillment is more sustained than anything I have ever been involved in for an extended period.

8. What do you think makes a good friend?

In my estimation, a good friend is someone who supports you in the hard times, advises you in the challenging times, comforts you in times of crisis, and holds you accountable when you need it. A good friend is someone you can count on more than anyone else, even some family members. They are loyal—sometimes to a fault—and defensive of you when others offend you. A good friend is rare, cherished, and for many people elusive.

9. What's your biggest life lesson so far?

The main thing I have learned through coming to prison is no amount of money can yield true happiness—only meaningful relationships can provide this. Prior to coming to prison, I constantly chased superficial things (money, luxury cars, women, fancy clothes), believing they would bring me a heightened level of happiness, self-importance, and validation. They never did. Now, however, it's receiving a letter, birthday card, Christmas card, and visits that fill me up with joy and self-esteem, knowing people thought I was important enough to do these things for me. This lesson has given me a greater appreciation for the things that truly matter in life, and I hope to never lose sight of this truth when my time is up in this dreaded place.

10. What advice would you give to your younger self or to a child in a similar position as you were when you were young?

Please see the blog post I wrote at the end of this questionnaire entitled, "Letter to My Younger Self."

11. What does it feel like to live in prison?

To live in prison feels like living in a zoo. We live in cages, are guarded by the "zoo keepers" who also feed, clothe, punish, and reward us when warranted. We are not allowed to freely roam beyond certain points, must comply with every demand that is made of us, and are only set free when the zoo keeper says so. We are made to be content with our foreign homes, forced to create new "families" and friends with other captives, and are often dejected at the resignation that this is our new home with seemingly no end in sight. Visitors come in and their expressions convey their fear of the animals. They are instructed to not get too close lest they put themselves in harm's way.

12. How do you feel about the prison system or the justice system?

Clearly when you look at how the War on Drugs campaign that started in the 70s and the tough-on-crime era in the 90s have ballooned our prison system from 300,000 to over 2.3 million incarcerated, there is a crisis on our hands. The recidivism rate for the over 600,000 people who release from prison every year is 67% over a three-year period. When you account for the first five years of their release, it ticks up to over 70%. If the rate at which we incarcerate and give lengthy sentences to law breakers drastically reduced crime, rehabilitated, and therefore substantially reduced the recidivism rate, then critics of the status quo wouldn't have much of an argument—but obviously this is not the case. So if the model is not producing desirable results, what sense does it make to keep the model intact? Would a business do so if its model did not yield a profit?

The focus cannot simply be on locking people up and throwing away the key; there has to be a concerted effort to rehabilitate those who are, in many cases, living with and suffering from addiction, abuse, and mental health deficiencies. This will not only benefit the offender with a better quality of life but will certainly benefit the communities they return to as well because they will be law-abiding, tax-paying citizens.

13. What makes you laugh?

My fiancée is pretty funny, so we laugh a lot, and I also enjoy comedians such as Martin Lawrence, Cedric the Entertainer, and Kat Williams.

14. Finish the sentence:

If I could change the world, I would get people to magically see that we are much more alike than we are different. This, I believe, is the linchpin to eradicating racism, bigotry, and intolerance.

I believe life is ten percent what happens to you and ninety percent how you respond to it.

I wish people didn't have to suffer from poverty and cancer.

I am inspired by the reward in helping others, knowing I am making a meaningful difference in others' lives, often those who are forgotten by mainstream society.

15. Please share anything else you'd like. This is your space. And your voice.

Prior to coming to prison I assumed, like many, that everyone in prison was inherently bad, did extremely abhorrent things to get there, and should be there for as long as they were sentenced. It didn't take long after being here that I came to discover, by and large, people here are regular people who made a horrible decision—predominantly while under the influence of a chemical substance. This is not to excuse what they did, but it is to explain how the effects of addiction and untreated mental disorders can be catastrophic. The people here—now clean and sober—resemble most law-abiding, responsible people in society. This changed my skewed perception of those incarcerated, humanizing them in a way that, in turn, shone a glaring light on the inhumane ways in which we treat individuals who come into the justice system.

Thanks to people like you, Melissa, and countless other unsung heroes who see the inherent value in human beings—despite what the consensus may think—who are incarcerated, perceptions will slowly be challenged and biases will be broken down. Before people can care about prison reform, incarcerating at a much lower rate, and fair sentencing practices, they must first see us as humans deserving of compassion and correction simultaneously. The work you are embarking on will aid that effort. Thank you.

Letter to My Younger Self
by Martin Lockett

Dear Martin,

I write to you from the other side—the side that awaits you if you don't change your course of action soon.

I know you are going through an extremely difficult time right now as you seek independence while trying to figure out your identity. Most teenagers find themselves doing the same thing. Your friends are very influential right now, and I understand that no one wants to be shunned by their peers, but please believe me when I say what you have been doing to impress them and gain acceptance is NOT who you are and will only lead you down a path of self-destruction.

I know you started drinking because you are very shy and wanted to come out of your shell, but if you knew what I know, you'd stop right now. You wouldn't pick up another drink if you knew you would become a full-blown alcoholic within the next two years; if you knew your alcoholism would eventually cause you to tragically take two innocent lives by drinking and driving, leading to a seventeen-and-a-half year prison sentence! Martin, you're better than that! You're smarter than that and can make it in this world by pursuing what makes you happy—not what others want or expect from you.

You have so much potential. I see it beneath your bravado, tough-guy exterior. You don't have to put up this facade with me—I know you…better than you will ever know! You're not a gangster, thug, or tough guy—who are you kidding? No, you're passionate about art and writing, so why not pursue those with everything in you? Trust me, you will not regret taking this path in life; it sure beats the alternative—the one that surely awaits you if you stay on the destructive path you're currently on.

Man, if you only knew the pain you're putting your mom through by going to jail for those stolen car escapades you and your brother have been going on with your so called friends. Are you crazy?! You're already putting yourself in a category that makes it more likely you'll end up in prison than college! How do you think your mom will feel about that? Believe me, Martin, her pain will be immense. In fact, it very well could contribute to her death some years from now! You don't want that on your conscience, do you? But imagine how happy she would be if you did what you've always talked about doing, going to college to be an architect.

You don't want to be where I am, where you'll be told when you can shower, use the phone, watch TV, eat, and go to bed. You don't want to miss your nieces and nephew's birthdays and Christmases for the next seventeen and a half years, do you? It is beyond dejecting to have to watch them grow up in pictures and visits every six months or so. Trust me, that would make you regret every decision you are currently making in your life, Martin.

There are countless men where I am who routinely reflect on their lives when they were your age, expressing how they wished they had made different choices that would have kept them from this dreaded place. I am amongst them. I pray you change soon so you're not counted among us as well. Change before it's too late!

I see what you and your friends do. Where do you think that will lead you? Seriously, I want you to take a moment and ponder where you think those things will get you. Do you think there is a future in doing drugs, drinking, and stealing? Look around you; name one successful alcoholic or drug addict! Listen, I'm not here to lecture you; I never liked that either when I was your age, but as I now sit here in a concrete cell staring out of a narrow window into a courtyard with a basketball hoop and barbed wire, a huge part of me wishes I had paid attention to what those older people were trying to tell me. Clearly they knew things I didn't, even though I thought I knew what I was doing. I only tell you these things because I love you and don't want to see you end up here—this dreaded place that surely awaits you if you keep on your treacherous path. They even already have a number assigned to you if and when you show up here!

I want you to reject what those who claim to be your friends want you to do because when you really think about it, you should be able to see they don't have your best interest at heart. Be true to yourself, believe in yourself, and give yourself a chance—you deserve it. Deny these people the opportunity of ever being able to use that state inmate identification number—ever!

Love,
Your Older Incarcerated Self

May 6, 2018

Martin,

I was so touched by your responses to my "Share Your Voice" questions that I had to write to thank you.

Your response came a day before the launch party for my second book, and I was preparing to give a talk and a reading from my book for the event. When I read your "Letter to My Younger Self," I felt buoyed by your spirit. You wrote to yourself: "I know you're passionate about art and writing, so why not pursue those things with everything in you?" I felt your wisdom, your artistry, your purpose, and your desire and it spoke to me at just the right moment—a call to shake off all my efforts to play it small or step out of the spotlight and to rise into my power, my authenticity. To claim myself.

And what I felt about you when reading your words is you are, most certainly, a writer. But, more than that, you are a healer and a visionary. You are a man who acts with purpose.

I cannot wait to get a copy of your book *Palpable Irony*. I promise to write back when I do.

With much gratitude,
Ashley

May 10, 2018

Dear Ashley,

Thank you very much for your wonderful, thoughtful, and kind words. I'm glad to know my responses were adequate. Please feel free to ask if you want me to elaborate further. I'm an "open book."

I was really touched that you'd be inspired by my blog on the eve of such a monumental event when you were obviously gathering your own thoughts and presentation points. So I have to know, how did it go? I have no doubt that it was very much a success because, well, it looks like that's kinda been your track record. :)

Have you always been inspired to write? I didn't graduate from high school, so I'll be the first to tell you I absolutely never thought of myself as a writer, although there was always something within me, despite my struggles, that made me feel I could do and be more than I was showing. But you'll read about my adolescent woes in *Palpable Irony*. I appreciate the fact that you'd be interested in knowing my life story—thank you, Ashley. I hope you enjoy it.

I must admit that I've never been called a "healer" and "visionary"—wow! Thank you. That's high praise that I'm not sure I have earned, but I'll take it. I find that I'm more and more comfortable with living in my new identity, and even though compliments such as yours are still relatively new, I'm telling myself to accept them, own them, live them. I definitely know things don't happen by mere happenstance, so my purpose is what drives me and keeps me centered in such a chaotic place.

I could talk for pages and ask a million questions, but I won't do that to you! I know you already have pen pals that keep you busy in whatever little free time you may have, so I'm not asking you to take on another. However, if and when you feel the urge to write, you may.

Thanks again for reaching out to me to thank me for my contribution to your project, but you're the one who needs to be thanked for giving voice to the voiceless. Best wishes with everything, Ashley. We'll talk when we talk!

Sincerely,
Martin

June 6, 2018

Martin,

I've been reading your book for a week now and I'm half-way through. I think what I most love is now, when I re-read your letter to me in your own handwriting, I feel like I know you. Like I recognize the boy I've been reading about. I feel you closer, brought to life.

I think it's bold and brave that you've chosen to share your story in a book. That you're so willing to express yourself and allow others to hear you. When I published my most recent book, a reader told me it was "brave" for me to write as I did, "vulnerably," she said. It's funny because that had never crossed my mind when writing it or publishing it: I didn't find it particularly bold or brave or even vulnerable. I simply wrote what I did because I had an overwhelming feeling to write—to unleash what's within.

But now that I read your words, I recognize your bravery: you have pushed up against so many limits in order to create *Palpable Irony*. I admire your refusal to be denied your own voice.

So, yes, I carried your spirit with me to my book launch. I felt so nourished by it, by everyone who came to support me. I felt the room, the silence dropping as I spoke—it was an honor to be heard, to be listened to so intently. I loved all the little girls in the room—all under 9 years old —who sat so patiently and kindly as I spoke. And it was a reminder of my own passion: getting to fill the room with my words and be filled with the spirits of those who chose to attend reminded me that this is what I love most

—the communing that comes when we allow ourselves to be seen, fully and raw.

I'm glad you've chosen to receive my compliments and love what you wrote: "I'm more and more comfortable living with my new identity…I'm telling myself to accept them, own them, live them." That's powerful advice. Yes, keep owning your gifts (I know you have many) and sharing who you are from your soul.

Lastly, feel free to write as often as you'd like and ask as many questions of me as you'd like! It's only fair—I did send a two-sided sheet to you with questions about yourself. ;) I'm open to answering any of yours.

If you'll permit me: one more question. I'd love to know more about your fiancée. It seems she helped bring your book to life? Tell me about her and how you met. What does it feel like to have her in your life? I've been writing rather openly lately about seeking my own partner and, so, I want to hear what empowered and loving relationships feel like. What moves you most about being with your fiancée?

In friendship,
Ashley

June 13, 2018

Dear Ashley,

So good to hear back from you!

I'm so grateful and delighted that you are reading and enjoying my book, that you feel like you know me more now that we're corresponding. I *have* to read your most recent one now so I can feel the same. I, as you can imagine, debated back and forth in my head whether or not I would include certain things in my book that rendered me 100% vulnerable and gave people another side of me that I'm not very proud of. But I made up my mind that I would be 100% honest about who I was and who I am because anything less would be inauthentic. And I learned long ago that an omission is still a lie, and a "half-truth" is a whole lie. So if I was going to write my story, it would be *my* story. I think people (like you) appreciate authenticity over anything else, so I'm glad I wrote it the way I did. And it was truly cathartic, which I didn't expect.

Since you didn't particularly feel "brave" or "bold" when writing your second book, it must have come fairly easy— or natural—to express yourself, huh? Have you always been very expressive and open? No fear? As you read, I used to be terribly shy, which is why I still find it ironic to be doing speeches with ease and confidence. But this is who I am, this is what my purpose is. And clearly you are born to write and express!

What I wouldn't have given to be at your book launch party, Ashley. It sounded so amazing, so captivating. People were obviously entertained and intrigued with your words, your voice, and I would have loved to be there to listen and support another independent author. New York is on my list to visit, so maybe I'll one day get my opportunity to sit in the crowd and hear you share yourself with the room.

So I had a few guys from here send you their "Share Your Voice" responses. I'd also sent one to my buddy, Eric Burnham, at another prison, and he told me he'd actually heard from you and was corresponding with you, so I'm glad you have his writing because, as you now know, he's a strong writer. If you need more voices, I'd be glad to hand out more. I'm excited to see it all come together, to see you work your magic!

Ask as many questions as I'd like? Alright, you asked for it! First, do I get a picture to see who I'm writing? How old are you? Any children? Any siblings? Have you lived in New York your whole life? Do you like it? You mentioned writing about "seeking [your] own partner"— how so? How are you going about seeking a partner? Do you feel lonely at times? What's the most difficult thing you deal with living in NY? Are your parents around? How did you start your business? Alright, I'll stop with the interrogation now.

You asked about my fiancée—I have no problem answering any questions you have about our relationship. You will likely have already read about how we met and who she is, so I'll just answer your other questions.

What does it feel like to have her in my life? I'm not sure I can adequately do it justice in words, but I'll say she is the best thing that ever happened to me. She has instilled a sense of belief in myself that I hadn't had prior to knowing her. She has shown me what true love looks like and feels like, enabling me to reciprocate and know what it feels like to love in return. Prior to her, I'd been extremely selfish and superficial, as you've read. You know you have met the "right one" when that person makes you want to become the best version of yourself you can be.

Well I'll wrap this up here. Thank you so much for taking the time to write, Ashley. Thank you for your kind, sincere words of encouragement, and I look forward to getting to know you better—and reading your book!

Truly,
Martin

June 18, 2018

Martin,

It brought me so much joy to open your letter and find photos inside. Thank you for sharing you and your graduation with me. Once again, you've given me that personal touch of you. So I wanted to do the same. Enclosed, as I'm sure you've already found, are photos of me.

In fact, you wrote in your letter that you think people (like me) appreciate authenticity. That's what I see from you, in your photos and in your words. I can also sense how purposeful you are. Just as you so kindly wish to sit in the audience of one of my book readings one day, I wish to sit in one of yours—to hear you lead in your speeches. Just from your photos, I can feel your charisma.

Like you, I was often shy when I was younger, but I expressed myself through words readily. In other words, I wasn't the type to go up to anyone and just start talking or playing with other kids. But, at home, I spoke a lot and I was always writing and inventing—designing and sewing clothes (my oh-so-patient little dog had quite an extensive wardrobe!), painting, making jewelry, etc.—as a way to express myself. But was I fearless? No. I think as I've gotten older (I'm 28, to answer your question), I've learned to release myself more. Not to hold back. To be exactly who I am, whether that's "different" or not. I imagine I will only continue to learn and grow into myself. I want to uncover all parts of me.

Let me add to that my thanks: thank you for sharing your voice on Adopt an Inmate and for spreading the word about my project. Yes, I have received several letters from men in Oregon and am grateful for all of them. And I love that you're friends with Eric! He's a fantastic writer and seems like a really great guy. You have that in common.

So let me answer your questions:

1. Any children?
No children. I spent four years in college babysitting almost nightly and working at an amazing nursery school where I learned so much. But I don't think I want my own kids. I'm hoping for a niece or nephew some day (or both!) and to serve the world's children in other ways.

2. Any siblings?
Yes, one older brother, Steven. Though our personalities are different, he has always been a connector for me, often unknowingly bringing me to the people and places I most needed. He is cautiously adventurous, if that combination exists, a touch sarcastic and very witty, and sometimes uncertainly but also bravely trying to follow a less trodden path.

3. Have you lived in NY your whole life? Do you like it?
I was born in Lexington, KY, actually. Then moved to Long Island, then Boca Raton, FL, and then back to New York. I've been living in New York since I was 6 years old. I spent four years during college in Manhattan, and have since returned to the suburbs. I would like to go back to the city, mainly to connect to like-minded individuals and to keep learning—there are more opportunities there to attend lectures, sermons, book readings, yoga classes, etc.

4. How am I seeking my partner?

I have lasted about a week on dating apps. Even the thought of them makes me feel restricted. I don't want to "swipe" a photo left or right to determine chemistry; I want someone who wants to go deeper. I've also found the dating pool on there to be devastatingly un-stimulating. (I get that generalizing is unfair. I'm sure there are men on those apps with substance and wit.) I want someone purposeful, a leader, an advocate. So my search is largely in my heart: I remain open. I seek him by living my purpose. By believing I'm worthy of meeting my match. By not settling. By expressing all of me. I believe that is the only way I will attract him. Other than that, I am relying on fate. When it's time, he will come.

5. Do I feel lonely at times?

Yes.

Do you?

6. What's the most difficult thing I deal with living in NY?

Traffic lol.

7. Are my parents around?

Yes, and I'm especially close with my mom who listens to me with patience and love, including through moments of darkness and pain. I'm grateful for her.

8. How did I start my business?

I never intended to create a skincare line. In fact, it was the last thing I would have imagined for myself. In college, my skin began breaking out in these angry, red bumps. I ate really healthy, so I knew it wasn't from food. I would take trips every weekend to Whole Foods Market and pick up a new natural skin cream to try to see if it would calm my broken-out skin. I had given up taking prescription or even over-the-counter medication when I was in middle school. Desperate, though, I went to the dermatologist and broke my vow: I tried a medication.

Nothing worked.

Somehow, I got the idea to try creating my own skin elixirs. So I read as much as I thought I needed and then trusted my intuition and created my first skincare products in my dorm room kitchen. To my delight, it worked.

Still, I didn't plan on pursuing it. But, in the months after creating my line, I would have people stop me on the street, on line at the store, etc. and say, "You have such beautiful skin. What do you use?" I would tell them, "I make my own," and they'd ask, "Can I buy it?" I'd just shrug my shoulders and say, "No," as if I thought the idea was ridiculous.

It must have been a calling, though, because a few years later, I finally launched my own organic line. What I am certain of, though, is that this line is not about beauty as the mainstream industry promotes it. It is about beauty that stems from peace. That stems from love. In fact, I wrote this on my skincare website's blog the other day, as I imagined the impact of my work beyond those who can afford it:

> What I am, then, is an advocate for beauty—which means I am an advocate for social justice because human rights and equality and fairness are beauty. Which means I am an advocate for our earth because a sustainable, life-giving planet is beauty. Which means I am an advocate for intuition

because beautiful things arise when we listen to our instincts. Which means I am an advocate for kindness and community and peace because that is beauty, too.

What is also beauty is the way you described your relationship with your fiancée—her presence in your life inspires you to fulfill yourself, to be your highest version.

To end, I will tell you that I sent a copy of my book *The Moon and Her Sisters* from Amazon to you. Usually, it arrives in a day or two but, for some reason, it's showing the expected delivery time as one week.

I would love to hear back from you. Do tell me: what have you spent the most time thinking about lately? Do you follow current events? I've been reading and watching about the children whose parents come seeking asylum or freedom from violence and who are being separated from them at the border. Infuriating and outrageously tragic don't even do it justice.

In friendship,
Ashley

June 26, 2018

Dear Ashley,

Hey! Wow! Thank you for the awesome pictures! It's so nice to put a face with the name! I love that I get to see different aspects of you in each of them. In the one where you're petting the rescue animal, I get to see you in nature, showing compassion for who and what needs it most. And this one with your precious grandma is my favorite—so adorable. She is your heart and I know you are hers. Thank you for sharing her with me. Lastly, this one of you doing what probably only five other people on planet Earth can do is amazing! You are deceptively strong, Ashley. So petite, yet so strong and fierce in so many ways.

I'm glad you liked mine as well. Even though you didn't ask for them, I wanted to send them. If and when I feel like someone is going to be in my life for a long time, I like to send pictures from time to time.

I appreciate that you'd want to sit in at one of my book readings one day, but first I'll need some pointers from you—the pro! I'd love to see how you draw in the crowd, use voice inflections to capitalize on their intrigue, take them on the journey with you step-by-step. I'm pretty decent at speeches, but book-reading is a different form of artistry, right? Did you see my Dr. King commemoration speech on YouTube? I'll be doing one on Rosa Parks in August. My panel speech was also emailed to every DUI panel coordinator across your state. I'll be going to NY to speak publicly at panels when I get out. I'd love to see you at one of them.

Speaking of your expression, looks like I'll have two copies of your book! I ordered it about a week ago. Thank you very much for sending a copy, as well. I'll donate a copy to the library. I'm excited to read it. I feel like I'll feel when you read mine—that I *really* know the person I'm writing. Not that you haven't been forthcoming about yourself—you have. You know what I'm saying, though. Our writing comes from the deepest part of ourselves—our thoughts, fears, passions, insights, and our soul. I look forward to reading your resonant words.

Have you read Michelle Alexander's *The New Jim Crow?* Phenomenal! I've got reviews for it on Adopt an Inmate's website. I love reading books that will change my perspective on important issues or bolster my perspective on them. I am a critical thinker, so I like to know why I feel a certain way about something, not just accept my emotions as rationale.

Speaking of important matters, yes, I stay up on current events on my 13" TV in my cell. Those poor children being torn from their families is the most cruel, abhorrent, disgusting thing I've seen in a long time. This president (still grappling with even giving him that title) and his administration are antithetical to everything America espouses to be. Anyway, it's just a sad situation all around. I just hope he's outvoted in 2020.

So is Steven there? You two seem close and share a special sibling bond. Does he think you've totally lost your marbles sharing yourself with inmates? Hey, who could blame him? :)

I'm sorry your experiences thus far on the dating sites have been, um, underwhelming. Sadly, I'm not surprised this has been the case for you because you are a very different type of woman than what guys on those sites are used to. It's not to say there aren't sophisticated, professional, bright women on there—I'm sure there are.

At the same time, I'd hate to see you give up so soon and possibly miss an incredible man you would not have otherwise met, fell in love with, and lived happily ever after. I'm glad you're keeping your heart open, Ashley, because it would be a shame if you deprived someone from being able to experience that with you and for you to deprive yourself of that life-changing love. As long as you keep living your purpose, as you said, I have no doubt that you will attract a like-minded man that will complement you and vice versa. You're definitely worthy of meeting your match—and you will!

Do I feel lonely at times? Of course I do. I feel lonely plenty of nights when I'm going to bed, or on Christmas, Thanksgiving, some birthdays, etc. It helps knowing I have people outside who love me, but they're not in here with me. When the lights go out—it's me and my thoughts.

What I've been thinking about the most lately is my freedom—going to the beach and letting the water run over my feet as I walk along the edge. I think about making passionate, exhilarating love to my girl, eating strawberry pancakes with whipped cream and scrambled eggs for breakfast, visiting the Statue of Liberty. I often think about getting on an airplane for the first time, taking an Uber for the first time, struggling to learn my way around a smart phone, the Internet, and applying for work online. I don't have enough paper to enumerate all the things I have been thinking about lately, but we have time, don't we?

Well, my new friend, I'll leave it here. Thank you for the pictures and a beautiful letter. I hope to hear from you soon.

Always,
Martin

July 1, 2018

Dear Ashley,

I started to wait to write you until I received your next letter, but I feel compelled to write right now as I just finished your book *The Moon and Her Sisters* five minutes ago! In a nutshell: soothing to the soul, energizing to the spirit, captivating to the mind, heartwarming to the, well, the heart. In full disclosure, I've never been a big fan of poetry because it's usually too abstract and over my head; it never resonated because I had to try too hard to uncover the essence of what was being conveyed, but not with yours. I hung on to every word, eager to read on and having my interpretation confirmed with the caption at the end. I'd like to talk about a few of the lines that especially resonated with me and why. Truthfully, I could say something about all 113 pages and their eloquent messages, but I'll spare you.

"The moon does not stop being and exercising its power even in darkness, so why should I question mine?" (6). Indeed, this is my mentality. In fact, I think we shine our brightest in our darkest hours because that's when we rely on our resilience, our ability to discover parts of ourselves that would have never been brought to the surface had the darkness never come.

"Want to see a family, a community, a nation thriving? You will see them honoring the wellbeing of their women" (10). My words are not needed here, but I'll add them anyway. Women are the bearers of life, the nurturers of growth, and the backbones of our families. And I think you are 100% correct—how well nations and communities do is directly linked with how well they treat their women. We could certainly use more women in positions of power—namely Congress—so more could get done for the benefit of us all.

"I can give you a list of excuses why it's not happening for me, but none rival the lies I tell myself about what's impossible" (12). It reminds me of one of my AA coins that says, "I seek strength not to be greater than my brother but to fight my greatest enemy—myself." If we spent half the time we spend on making excuses and lying to ourselves about what's possible or not on exerting effort into our goals, we'd surprise ourselves. I've come to discover that myself during this time, but it didn't come overnight. We have to first fight off all the negative self-talk that's come so naturally over the years due to others instilling it or how we've come to see ourselves for a variety of reasons.

"I just wanted to remind us: every shape and way of being is tempting, not because it's your job to be desirable, but because the form you come in was ordered up by God and that's madly rousing" (18). How essential that self-acceptance is. Sadly, however, we're (mainly women and little girls) constantly swimming against a current of body-image conformity that is largely propagated by the media.

"…Your energy is greed, which is a guise for the enemy of not feeling you're enough" (22). Now let me first say I thought this poem was spot-on in identifying the president's true weaknesses and how they manifest in the travesty of a presidency that we have before us. The reason why this particular line on greed resonated is because it was me. I felt wholly inadequate and felt I had to cover it up with superficial items and objects to make up for it—it never worked. Greedy people, in my opinion, suffer, to some degree, from the same basic inadequacy. If only they knew the key to their happiness and sense of importance and meaning would come not from hoarding things but from giving it away to help others.

"When a mountain stands before you, instead of asking, 'Why me?' think: 'This is an invitation.' Let me grab my boots and begin climbing…—*this is your mountain: meet it*" (73). This is my mountain and I've chosen to climb it with fervor and resolve. I've taken away its power to intimidate and emasculate and used it to strengthen, wisen, and discover myself. Indeed, obstacles equal opportunities. I will forevermore approach all of life's adversities with this advantageous mindset.

"Don't ask me what I'll do if chasing my dreams fails, when all I want to ask you is what will you feel if you never try following yours?" (90). I love this one. I used to be too timid to try new things for fear of failing or looking dumb. How limiting it was. Like Pitbull says, "Reach for the stars and, if not, at least you'll fall on top of the world."

Once again, I thoroughly enjoyed every page of your book, Ashley. You are a very talented writer and I admire your courage and ability to inspire and motivate people of all kinds, especially young girls. I feel privileged to know you and have the opportunity to know more of you. I look forward to hearing from you soon.

Always,
Martin

July 6, 2018

Martin,

My plan for today was to respond to your letter, and then I received a second blessing from you in the mail, the letter you wrote after reading my book. The timing was divine and your words touched my soul. I think one of the best gifts you could offer me, as a writer, is to engage with my words, to tell me how they felt to you. To let me, for a moment, see my words through your eyes. And it feels like you read my words so carefully, that you were gentle with them, nurturing. I feel loved and seen by the way you responded. Thank you for caring for the words that rise from my soul.

The other thing I loved about that letter is the way you described darkness, that "we shine our brightest in our darkest hours because that's when we…discover parts of ourselves that would have never been brought to the surface had the darkness never come." In the moments I struggle with the path I walk, I will remember this: the darkness is making me shine brighter.

Martin, I just paused this letter for 20 minutes to watch your DUI Victim Impact statement. Wow. There's a lot anyone could say in response to this video, but all I will say is this: you are fulfilling your mission. I wish change didn't have to stem from two deaths and you trading 17 and half years of your own life, and I would like to say that in the wake of the crash is pure devastation. But it is not, because you are the glimmer. It is as if you were destined to speak, measured and powerful, altering the trajectory, hopefully, of many other lives.

The way you counted down what those who died in the crash may have been thinking 10 minutes, 5 minutes, 1 minute before the crash drew me in and slowed down time until I could feel them, thinking. Until I could imagine myself in their shoes. Until they had a human face in my mind.

And, of course, your story turns on that prophetic line: "Perhaps the person they will have helped the most is the man who's charged with their murder."

And then the 15 year old daughter of one woman who died grabbed my heart: "Mr. Lockett, I forgive you."

It is not enough to say you are a powerful speaker or that the situation is tragic. Your story had me mourning their lives, and feeling yours. It had me mourning for your mother and the fiancé of your victim and for his son whose father was so devastated and angry. It left me sad and empowered. It left me speechless, for once, and wanting to say everything, maybe just to make noise because words cannot even do it justice.

And, even more than before, it left me wanting to call you my friend. I will share this video. And I want to be in the audience someday soon when you deliver this speech. I want to feel you, coming powerfully with your truth, and I want to feel the room.

I planned on writing to you about other things in your letter, about the way you described longing for your freedom so deliciously that I could feel it. And about my brother—yes, we are close, and I don't think he thinks I've lost my marbles writing to people like you. If anything, I think he secretly likes it, that I am who I am and that I do what I do. And about *The New Jim Crow,* which I picked up from the library this morning with you in mind.

But you've left me taking everything in from that video, just being in it for a moment. And, so, it seems there's no more room to write.

Looking forward to more.

Always,
Ashley

Ernest

Eleven.

June 19, 2018

1. Introduce yourself! Tell me a little about you:

My name is Ernest L. Young Sr. I'm from Norfolk, Virginia and am somewhat of a loner. I guess that one could say I keep it true to a Scorpio's character. I'm old school; raised by my great grandmother along with great aunts and great uncles by the old school playbook.

2. Describe what you look like. What do you like about how you look? Is there something you wish you could change?

I am a brown man, tall in stature, with strong African and Native American features. I like the pronounced structure of my cheekbones. I would not change anything about myself. I represent my ancestors.

3. Do you have family? If so, tell me about them.

The elders I was raised by have all gone forward during the time of my incarceration. My children remain, though, in my absence and without access to right knowledge. They have not grown with family values.

4. Do you have children? If so, what do you most love about them? What do you miss about them?

I have six children. I love and miss everything about them.

5. What are your goals?

My one goal in life is to leave behind proof that I lived...
that I did exist.

6. If you could leave prison for a day, what would you do?

If I could leave prison for one day, I would like to ride a
bicycle through my old neighborhood for an hour or so
before it wakes up. I envision a perfect spring morning,
one where the temperature is just right and the sweet
aroma of spring blooms mask over the foul stench of my
ghetto. The time from sunrise until sunset would be spent
with my children. And if I'm fortunate enough to have a
trusted lady friend or wife, the remainder of my freedom
would be spent awake with her.

7. Do you believe your life has a purpose or specific mission? What is it?

I do believe my life has a purpose. I count my blessings
nightly. And when I tally up all the times I've lived while
those around me perish, I know my life is a mercy and
that I'm above ground for a reason. I'm left to believe
that I'm the scribe. And I live to tell the tale of our war,
giving detailed accounts of every battle, told from a first
hand point of view.

8. What do you think makes a good friend?

What makes a good friend is selflessness and loyalty.

9. What's your biggest life lesson so far?

My biggest lesson in life is that it's never too late to become who you might've been. Because sometimes we find our destinies on the path we took to avoid it.

10. What advice would you give to your younger self or to a child in a similar position as you were when you were young?

The advice I'd give to my younger self, and what I give to my children, is to see people and things as they are, not as they ought to be. Be fearless. If you want to get to the other side of a thing you must remove all doubt, then commit to the jump.

11. What does it feel like to live in prison?

Life in prison is painful. That's the all of it.

12. How do you feel about the prison system or the justice system?

Justice, "Just ice," is a cold game. With rules that apply only to men who stand up, those who refuse to snitch, and the poor.

13. What makes you laugh?

—

14. Finish the sentence:
If I could change the world, I would do away with modern science and technologies and declare that all of humanity should reclaim simpler times and ways of life.

Before people had everything at their finger tips—before everyone had all the damn sense, there was a pecking order and the world had more balance and harmony. Today it's every man, woman, and child for themselves. Once upon a time, truth, right, and good advice was worth more than gold. Now cash rules EVERYTHING. The world needs simpler times to give it time to heal.

15. Please share anything else you'd like. This is your space. And your voice.

I am also a writer. I write about the human condition from a real and honest standpoint.

I appreciate what you and those like you do for us exiled and, more times, forgotten souls. Many of us have no voice, though we all have something to say. We're counted amongst the dead. We live like ghosts. You have a gift. You can see us; you can hear us. I'm grateful.

Ernest L. Young, Sr.

June 25, 2018

Ernest,

When I read your words, I hear your warrior spirit. And I don't mean the type of warrior who roots himself in violence or destruction. I mean the warrior whose spirit is his weaponry, who lives with valor and courage. You write with a clarity that is bold and assertive without impinging upon any other living thing: you speak truth.

Your existence is defiance: as those around you perish, you gather those passed souls and rise with them, as if your voice and leadership is made stronger by a long line of ancestors who stand tall, in spirit, with you. And I think that's what I loved most about your description of your physical self: "I would not change anything about myself. I represent my ancestors."

The color and features of your body has (ludicrously and ignorantly) been made grounds for denigration and dehumanization by men and women too weak to understand that we are linked, that we are made stronger by each other. And, yet, here you are, declaring yourself: "I am brown," you write, owning your skin.

I was listening to a comedian last night, Hannah Gadsby, who masterfully weaved her story, including traumas and anger and vulnerability and resilience, into her performance and she said that self-hate comes from the outside (we do not naturally grow it within ourselves) but, once it has been implanted in us, often from childhood, it is nearly impossible to rewire ourselves and grow the seeds for self-worth. It is hard, she said, to flourish. I see you upending that, not allowing falsely planted shame to take root. I admire you because so many of us fight with ourselves daily, attacking ourselves with our own words and thoughts about who we are or who we think we should be or whether we are good enough as we are. You inspire us to claim our bodies and claim our selves and declare our worth. We deserve to take up space.

So when you write that you are the scribe, I know it. I feel it in my bones which are made from the earth, which is where we all begin and all end: recycled. And, so, when you talk about the "tale of our war," I sense you, the stories you are here to tell. But I have not lived it like you. Tell me, what do you mean when you speak of battles?

You acknowledge my gift to see "the dead," the "forgotten souls," and for that I am honored and grateful. But you have made it so easy. You come powerfully; I would have to be so utterly disconnected not to see you, not to feel you. And I guess herein lies our problem: when you write of simpler times, you write of "balance and harmony." That is what is lost: our tethers to each other and to our planet. So rarely do we root our bare feet in the earth and feel each other. This is our downfall. Still, I believe we can rise.

With respect,
Ashley

June 29, 2018

Ashley,

your words are powerful. not since the time of my great grandmother has such strong reasoning been directed towards me. her words spoke things into existence. I compare you to her. with your words my chest and back is broader—my back straighter—I'm taller. I have waited for you.

we come from different worlds and now find ourselves sharing space in the vast universe. it was only a matter of time that travelers headed in the same direction should cross paths. the universe has conspired to make it so. but not before life and experience has prepared us for one another's energy.

you interest me. people find one another everyday, but it's a rare occasion when individuals meet: not just in passing and headed in different directions, but going the same way. you're special. I don't yet know the how, or why—I only know that you are. tell me more about yourself, a little of your back story. what part of the world does your last name come? where did you grow up? from where does your knowledge, wisdom, and overstanding come? who influenced your thinking the most?

to answer your question: what is the meaning of telling "the tale of our war"? myself along with several cousins and uncles are the sons of lost generations that came before us. our parents fell victim to the crack and AIDS epidemics. we were for the most part left to fend for ourselves. we lived in a slum. where everything was a survival thing. whatever a man got for himself he had to fight to get, and he had to fight even harder to keep it.

not all squabbles were physical. indeed the most violent battles were fought in the mental, and behind the chest: when sanity held on by a measly thread, and loss hurt so bad that it takes the breath away.
who lives must at some point fight for life. "our war."

my next response will be prompt. last week was the institution's annual lock down. we came up today.

Respect,
Ernest

July 7, 2018

Ernest,

Your email came to me early in the morning on July 5th, almost a week after you sent it to me. But I do not mind the delay because it came to me powerfully. I opened it on my phone and read it sitting on the floor, leaning up against my bed, which is perfect because I don't think I could have stood up reading it: like you, it struck me.

All this tension had been building up in my body all week and, when I read it, I cried.

I cried because, when you compared me to her, your great grandmother, I felt her in me and it's as if I saw her smiling at me with a look in her eyes that said, "I see you," and "I know who you are." And I felt her connecting me to my roots—ancient, to all the strong, wise women who came before me and who put their bets on me, who poured themselves into me to make me better, to make me stronger, to make me more equipped to continue their legacy.

I cried when you wrote, "It was only a matter of time that travelers headed in the same direction should cross paths," and I didn't realize why until I re-read it for maybe the tenth time now: because it felt like home. And I don't mean where I live but where I come from. I cried because I have been waiting for you, too, for souls destined to find mine. Because I have felt so lonely without them.

And, so, at the very least, I owe you answers to your questions. My last name comes from my father, whose family stems from Italy. I don't know what that means to me; I have never been there or met family that has grown or lived on that soil. Instead, I have felt my ancestry in the earth's soil and among the trees. I grew up, mostly, where I am now on Long Island, New York. There was nothing remarkable about it, nothing noteworthy. I grew up doing gymnastics far too much, going to my brother's baseball games on weekends and spending most of it doing handstands in the grass or reading while my mom sat beside me and my dad coached; I had grandparents who visited every summer from Florida and stayed for 6 weeks in our house, who took us for ice cream along the beach and tested my dad's patience! I ate boxed macaroni and cheese and hotdogs (which is still appalling to me as a plant-eater and wellness advocate now); and I had a family that loved me. But I suppose that last part is remarkable—the love.

Your letter keeps growing in me: I just saw it now, you used the word "overstanding." My "knowledge, wisdom, and overstanding" must come from the place I called "home." Whether my home is the same as yours, I do not know, but your overstanding must come from home, too.

I will answer your question about who influenced my thinking the most; first, I want to touch on your "tale of our war." But to do that, I must go back.

I must tell you about a former English teacher of mine. You talked about traveling in the same direction. He is one of the few people whose path I've crossed in this lifetime who has always made me feel like he's "going the same way."

I share this because, when I received your email and was struck by it, sitting on the floor, I sent some of your words to him.

He replied via text message: "My God: 'Who lives must at some point fight for life.' What a tremendous formulation of living. This might be my new mantra."

I wrote back, "'My God' is right."

In fact, I'm still trying to wrap my mind around what you wrote, of what it means to be "a son" of a "lost generation," of the incongruence between those two phrases. And I'm still trying to feel, to understand, "Whatever a man got for himself he had to fight to get, and he had to fight even harder to keep it." I keep trying to compare it to something in my life and I can't. It feels like something I don't know, like I'm struggling to grasp and, yet, I must know it. What have I had to fight for? I'm wondering. I feel wholly inadequate to even touch what you've written. Thank you for sharing it with me.

So I will return to your final question and, with it, to the woman whose books I have turned to for years: Alice Walker. I have found answers in my life simply by holding her books in my hands or up against my heart. She has expressed love like no other while recognizing with a fullness that she seems to know in her whole body the darkness.

Just so you can taste her, I will share a few of her lines. She opens one of my favorite of her books *We Are The Ones We Have Been Waiting For* with this, from Dickens: "It is the worst of times. It is the best of times." And she ends that very introduction like this:

To begin our long journey toward balance as a planet, we have only to study the world and its people, to see they are *so like ourselves! To trust that this is so.* That different clothes and religions do not create people who can escape from humanity. When we face the peoples of the world with open hands, and in honesty and fearlessness speak what is in our memories and our hearts, the dots connect themselves.

You may say to me: But Alice, all these connecting dots connect disasters. True enough, but they also connect millions of people who worked hard and beautifully to prevent, defeat, or transform them.

The best of times.

Ernest, I could ask questions of you in return, but I don't want to. I just want you to speak your mind.

With tremendous gratitude,
Ashley

July 9, 2018

Ashley,

out of many grands and great grand children, Emily
Cecilia Williams chose me to carry her name forward and
to be her proof. and so from the spirit world, she
conspires with my family's source to help me. the proof
of this is that I'm all that's left of her. among all that
remains of her, I am the only one who knows her smile.
her blood is strong in me. and through it, I can recall
firsthand accounts of the times when her mothers ruled.
I remember the fall: the middle passage. through my great
grand mother's blood memory, I can feel the masters
whip across our back. I know the fear. I feel the rage. I
can see my people hanged. I can smell their rotting flesh.

my Bigma has come to me every night since our
acquaintance. she doesn't say much, but she's happy,
which is odd for her, in life or death. so I say: somehow
you are special. my grandmother let you know her. she
knows who you are. she wants me to know you. normally,
I don't like to give people any part of me to hold on to. I
don't like to be pushed or pulled by peoples' intentions.
with you, though, I'm compelled to give to you whatever
part of me you might need.

love is remarkable, I suppose. I pray for her almost daily
and yet she continues to evade me. I wonder. in my
imagination I see myself and my queen inheriting the
earth with just she and I alone on the planet.

I know our connection. my family is from Brooklyn. the
wars I speak of took place mostly in East New York.
Queens was my get away, because Springfield gardens

reminded me so much of my Virginia slum. my brother's balcony in Rochdale was my favorite place to be. his balcony faced the Long island railroad where I would sit for hours watching the movements of the trains. it relaxed me. perhaps our souls have met then. and perhaps then it was set into stone that we would together find our destinies.

Ashley, who you are lets me know that you are and have been a fighter from birth. do not compare your load—your burden—to mine or to others' because you miss your life's lesson that way. a spoon full of poison has the same effect as a full cup, and so, a load is a load. everyone thinks he/she has a heavier load, but who feels it knows.

don't take away from your struggle. look at your life. see who you are, opposed to who you might be if you really were not a fighter. if you must compare, compare yourself to the many women amongst us who are lost beyond found. all those beautiful victims of whatever circumstance who know not their true birthright as queen and ruler. she is the strength of the world and the keeper of mankind, but knows not. she doesn't know her worth. you do know your worth. and you are fully aware of your birthright.

I love how I am able to feel you from afar. Another of your superpowers is telekinesis. You move a 216 pound man so easily. You're such a magician: so fluid with words. That you are who you are says to me that you are a fighter, and that you fight well. I am familiar with the jinn who roam those New York streets. my mother, her sisters and their daughters walked those streets. they were the direct descendants of the strongest woman I know. they too were strong, and yet not strong enough. use them to gauge your strength, Empress. your choice to disregard the bullshit and move towards a bigger judgement is a fight in and of itself. and not an easy one either. wear your victory with pride and continue to squabble.

I overstand how a soul can feel lonely amidst the masses. for my own part, and for most of my life, loneliness has been my constant companion. and I sometimes wonder how it is that I find myself alone in a vast universe atop a great big world? to me, the irony of the universe seems cruel. how those who are unworthy of good people, are often loved and surrounded by good people. while those who work to be better have nothing and no one. I never question what is and has to be, though the above remains a curiosity to me.

to over stand is a saying used by my family a lot. though I'm not all that sure which of my relatives started it. my heritage is a melting pot: African, East Indian, West Indian, and Asian. to overstand means that you have observed a thing from its best vantage point: a birds eye view, where one is allowed to see the fullness of a picture. you see more from above than from below.

Empress, there is nothing missing in the universe. we meet in the nick of time. only trust and honesty will reveal our purpose for one another. a purpose does exist. otherwise a total stranger would not have approached me and handed me your questionnaire. that is how we have been brought together. call it dumb luck, happenstance, chance, or destiny. whatever the case, it has been written. there is a chapter in your book of life and in mine that puts us together for some reason. We have come to that chapter. What will we do?

Respect,
Ernest

July 27, 2018

a poem from Ernest

Ashley,

I'm not a poet. Though, inspired by you, I'm moved to try my hand at the art of poetry. Read below:

I came in through a hole; a portal of a twelve year old.
a hole.
a hole is my part,
a hole is the love I seek; a hole is my heart.
my God! my soul!
a hole is my strife,
a hole is all I know lord; a hole is my life.
a hole is my breath,
a hole is my death.
when god roll call and the hole call. bury me. bury me as deep as I stood tall…in a hole.
a hole is all that's left.

Yours truly,
Ernest

Aubrey

Twelve.

ASHLEY ASTI

June 15, 2018

Hello Ms. Asti!

I am pleased to hear about your project, and would like to lend you a few of my thoughts to help in your endeavor. Originally, I was going to answer your questions in a common flow format. Much like a conversation or story would do. However that sauntering script didn't seem to fit your quick fired questions to my rambling gait. So, I'll answer them in kind and include my ramble afterwards for number fifteen.

1. Introduce yourself! Tell me a little about you:

My name is Aubrey "Michael" Hunter Dietrich Berryman. "You killed my father, prepare to die!" (Ya see, that's funny cause it's the Princess Bride. You get it. Of course you get it...don't you?) I am equal parts geek and gear-gripped jock. I have a quick mind, and sometimes to my detriment, a sharp tongue. I love to paint model miniatures one day, and go hiking the next. I enjoy sitting down to watch the game, and then going out to play on my own. In short, I believe myself to be a happy collection of walking contradictions. I might just be an original cliché.

2. Describe what you look like. What do you like about how you look? Is there something you wish you could change?

I am from a Germanic-Welsh heritage. In other words, I might be Bigfoot's twice removed, second cousin, on my father's side. Okay, so I'm not as hairy as an ape. I just happen to be built from similar stock, with a stripe of hair that runs from the top of my head to my ankles. Whatever, that's what they make Nair and razors for. I did inherit equal parts from my mother and father with the color of my eyes, as they are a blend of stormy blue sky over a grassy plane in August.

3. Do you have family? If so, tell me about them.

I have a family, and then I have family. One is a group I'd die for; the other is a collection of fair-weather friends that I share DNA or a name with.

4. Do you have children? If so, what do you most love about them? What do you miss about them?

I do not have any children. I could have at one point, but that opportunity has passed. When I am released at 47 years old, I will not have the time, resources, or inclination to even consider having children. Firstly, and this is a big one, I wouldn't have anyone TO have kids with. I'd be behind the ball and trying to get my life together, education, something resembling the start of a career, save money, plan for retirement (which I'll probably never be able to do), three years from over the hill. No, children are not in my future. I am great with kids. I adore my nieces and goddaughter. I can also give them back to their parents after a visit.

5. What are your goals?

I have a long list of goals that range through several spectrums. However, for the sake of expediency, I'll just name a few. I work in a silk screen industry, assigned to a computer workstation. On my desktop there are three clocks aside from the normal windows bar clock. Each clock is set to a different time zone, one for each of my special ladies. My niece, Moxie, is in San Diego; Dayna in Albuquerque; and Natalia, my goddaughter (aka Tali), lives in England. During my day I'll look at those clocks and see where they might be in their day, what they might possibly be likely to do at the present time. I imagine being able to make time for them, and the right time to do something special for them. As a prisoner, I am acutely aware of the passing of time. Yet like a ghost I am able to view the world, but unable to affect it in any manner. When I get out, I have a lot of time to make up, and in short order, too.

6. If you could leave prison for a day, what would you do?

If I could leave prison for a day, I'm not sure that I would. A day is just too short. It would be the worst tease, a reminder of what I once had. For a fleeting few hours, I would bask in all that possibility. Like a nightmare it would abruptly end, and I would still wake up in prison. No, thank you. I would not leave for a day. I couldn't take it.

7. Do you believe your life has a purpose or specific mission? What is it?

As a bit of an altruist, I do believe that my life has a purpose, albeit vaguely defined. It is like a shadow of an image, deep in a fog. While I can't quite make it out, I know what direction I have to walk. Yet the destination isn't the only goal. The journey is just as important, if not more so. What I do along the way will determine whether or not I'll be satisfied with my path and be able to look at myself reflected in the eyes of those I love.

8. What do you think makes a good friend?

I think a good friend knows when to listen, and when to talk. A good friend knows when to give, and when to take. And most importantly, a good friend knows when to lay a boot up the side of your head when you are about to do something amazingly stupid.

9. What's your biggest life lesson so far?

My biggest life lesson so far, shit…only one? All I know is that I don't know and that I have to be the change I want to see. I know that's technically two, but they're both equally important.

10. What advice would you give to your younger self or to a child in a similar position as you were when you were young?

If I could advise my younger self, I'd tell him to join the military. Get that damn GI bill and go to school. Don't be an ass-hat. No, taking a "gap year" isn't a good idea. If you had a daughter, how would you like her to be treated? Now, remember, that girl of yours is someone's daughter. Don't be a prick. You have two ears and one mouth for a reason. Your only limits are the ones you place upon yourself by the decisions you make. Lead don't follow. Invest in things that pay dividends, be it money or love, invest well.

11. What does it feel like to live in prison?

Prison is a lot like what I'd imagine a living purgatory is. You're not fully removed from the world, yet not part of it either. You might see or hear from family and/or friends, but damned if you could be there for them. You're a ghost, able to see but not touch. Once in a while, someone might hear you, but it usually stops there. There is a lot of wasted potential, time, life, love, and humanity flushed down a toilet. The boredom is beyond the pale of description and is the only thing besides misery that is plentiful. Days and weeks blend together in a blur of sameness. As you live them, it is painfully slow. Looking back the lens shifts, all of your days blend together as one. If prison could have a theme song, it would be Nine Inch Nails' "every day is exactly the same."

12. How do you feel about the prison system or the justice system?

The prison system is an industrial complex ever shifting to a total commercial enterprise under the guise of correction. There is no justice. Just us.

13. What makes you laugh?

I like to laugh, but I don't do it nearly enough. I most enjoy the ironic humor, or left field jokes. Sometimes a crude or crass joke is appreciated. I mean, whoever doesn't laugh at a fart or dick joke once in a while is just wound too damn tight. In my experience, it is those individuals that get targeted for pranks and have all manner of spontaneous "bad luck."

14. Finish the sentence:
If I could change the world, I would make people less selfish and more selfless. Everybody wins.

I believe that love and hate are the last magics. Your power comes from how you use them.

I wish that wishes spontaneously came true. However, it's people that bring the miracle.

I am inspired by conflict and contradiction.

15. Please share anything else you'd like. This is your space. And your voice.

Over the years, I have taken a certain amount of creative liberty writing about whatever my interest and passions have laid claim to. Those clever pieces of prose or poetic observations in no way make me a writer, much the same one is not a boxer after the first few jabs. I have only begun my training in the literal fight to lay words upon a body of experiences. I will more than likely spend my life in pursuit of mastery of an art that is as limitless as imagination. In my opinion, the only thing that comes close to giving voice to the ethereal emotions that convolute our hearts and minds is music. I should have been a better musician, maybe one day.

So imagine my chagrin when I was tasked with an inglorious subject, such as myself.

"Um, I don't typically write about myself, per se. It's normally my experiences and/or observations that catch my attention."

My taskmaster looked at me and smiled the way one does at a disfigured dog. He then said something so witty as to short-circuit my memory, yet the goal was indelibly left upon me. I had to write about myself, as a means of introduction. The intention was to humanize the vilified incarcerated individuals of a penal system that by and large is out of sight, and therefore out of mind from the general populace. Granted, there are some proper villains here. They *need* to be here. I myself may still be one of them. My own verdict has yet to return. The closing arguments were, after all, very compelling.

I have a quick wit, and a sharp tongue. It's a bit of a double-edged sword. I guess over a lifetime, a third of which has been incarcerated, one builds defenses. Sometimes I throw the silver a bit too readily, and cut those that least deserve it. I have been on both sides of that blade. Words can leave the deepest of wounds. They cannot be unsaid, and very seldom can more do any good. So I made a habit of humor, self-deprecating mostly. It seems to help with restraint. Between that and a good series of redundant mental filters to slam down upon wayward thoughts like a ten ton portcullis, I am not without my restrictions. then again, like the gaps in a portcullis, a few slide through from time to time.

I am, without a doubt, a massive underachiever. I have seldom lived up to my true potential. This was something that in hindsight must have been part of what made my parents disappointed in me so often. The real irony is that despite being part of a family that is as talented and articulate as we are, communicating effectively between parent and child is, at best, problematic. Simply put, we just don't know what to say to each other. When we did communicate, it was under a white flag of truce carried over eggshells. Our last parlay ended with minimal bloodshed, but with me ceding the war altogether. I was tired of the fight, the loss, the wounds and words that would never be gone. I simply walked away and never looked back. I believe it is better that way, because neither of us can continue to tear the other apart.

The lack of a coherent and communicating family body isn't a new development or one predicated on my crime. It was always there. During my younger years, I felt its lack on such a level that I didn't at first realize how I was building its replacement. Friends were the family I chose. My father would have called them "misanthropic misfits." My friends were a collection of oddballs, geeks, gearheads, and jocks. My girlfriend, Lelah, was my rock. I had no problem doing anything for my friends, for my family. I saw it as the only way. I still do. However in building my family I admitted a member that in hindsight I shouldn't have. He encroached upon my better nature. Throughout a series of events leading from one compromise to another, fueled by my obligation to family and friends alike, I soon found myself in a position I never before could dream of. I committed a terrible crime. In hindsight, it is all too similar to what happens with youth and the gangs that prey upon them. They offer a sense of security, family, and union. Then they twist it to their own means, whatever that may be. I was a follower, for a time. I had allowed this pied piper to lead me down the road to perdition, and have been paying for it ever since.

I will never be the follower that I was. I will lead with my own steps. I will be the change I want to see. Doing that here, in prison, is tough at times. It has to start somewhere, though. No one ever said it would be easy. Besides, if I can't do it here, I have no chance of making a difference out there. Maybe one day what I do can make a difference for someone, somehow, in some small way. That is part of the reason why I write after all. The change has to start somewhere. I hope to start it with a sentence. I hope those words bring thought. I hope that thought brings action. I hope that action brings change. I hope.

I give you permission to publish my words and my name.

A. Berryman

P.S. My sister built me a website for my work: www.wanderingwriting.com

P.P.S. I am very excited to hear your professional opinion. I'd like to pick your brain for experience in becoming an actual writer. (In my book, once you get published and paid, you're there!) I write all sorts of fiction/fantasy. However, my brother Ted thinks I should write about life and living here. I'm unsold, though. Who would buy another convict's story—just one—of waste? People are fickle readers, especially in this bubble gum pop-culture everything has to be fired rapid succession, Bam, Bam, Bam world. What you're doing is *awesome* and needs to be done. I'm sure others have attempted to do what you're doing. However, no one can do it like you. From what Taj tells me, I am a believer! "Be true to thy self." Do it your way, settle for nothing. Make your goal, and the message will fly. I will help in any way that I am able. I wish you only success and fortune in all your endeavors.

Best,
Aubrey "Bear" Berryman

July 2, 2018

Mr. Aubrey Berryman,

I think my favorite thing about your letter so far is the way you made me read it—the way your humor drew me in. The way your effortless way of expressing yourself made me move through it easily, so easily I almost didn't notice how great of a writer you are. And, most notably to me, the way I found myself jotting notes in the margins of your letter. That has always been my way of communicating with an author. The first books I fell in love with—by Alice Walker and Hemingway, Faulkner and Virginia Woolf—all called to me in their margins, the only communication I could have with them. I am lucky this time, though, because now I actually get to write back to you.

I marveled at the way you described your eyes—"a blend of stormy blue sky over a grassy plane in August," your playfulness with my life lessons question—"shit...only one?", and your leadership, both a statement and a call to action for yourself and for others: "I will lead my own steps. I will be the change I want to see...I hope that thought brings change." If you weren't certain whether you're a writer, let me assure you, you are. It is in you. I have no doubts.

And what I am thinking of now is this: last night, I listened to Adam Foss speak about incarceration. Foss is a former prosecutor who has left that job to found Prosecutor Impact, a non-profit organization that seeks to reshape the tools, education, and awareness every prosecutor has so that they understand the effects of their actions: so they know what it means to send someone to prison. He has charismatic eyes and an even more charismatic voice and spirit. For five years, he has been meeting with a group of men, many of whom have life sentences. And he spoke about it: it is easier for prosecutors (and all of us who don't feel tied to the prison system) to imagine that those we lock away aren't artists and writers and entrepreneurs and fathers and brothers and friends. And this is what you have written, too, of the "wasted potential"—"time, life, love, and humanity flushed down a toilet."

More than that, though, I share this because you exemplify what he's speaking of: tremendous talent. I read some of the website your sister put together and chose first the "Musings" section and, immediately upon entering it, the musing about bread. Which brings me back to what I wrote in the margins of your letter. First, I wrote, "humor," a way to remind myself to mention how you made me smile. Then something about Adam Foss, which we'll get back to. And then this last bit, about being "unsold" on the idea of writing about your prison experience. "Write what you're called to write," I scribbled back to you in the margins. "The call that comes from within, that comes from God. (It's the same call, anyway, isn't it?)"

This last thing I haven't had the guts to ask anyone else until I heard Adam Foss mention it in passing last night, and then you prompted me this morning as I read through your letter again. "You're a ghost," you told me about being in prison, "able to see but not touch. Once in a while someone might hear you, but it usually stops there." So, I want to know, what does it feel like not to be able to touch? Adam Foss had the guts to touch upon it (no pun intended) when he spoke last night, listing all the things men in prison are denied. He added to the list, "intimacy with a woman." I think touch is powerful and connecting. It connects us to ourselves, each other, to God or spirit or whatever you believe is higher than us or within us. And to be denied an intimate connection to a partner for sometimes many years, even a lifetime, must stunt us. Whether it's intimacy with a woman or a man, or even just petting a dog or giving a hug, our bodies and beings demand touch. At least, that's how I feel. I haven't asked anyone else about this, but I think you just may be bold enough, and sensitive enough, to answer.

Aubrey, I have been forward enough in asking questions of you. And you have been so gracious in sharing your voice with me. I honor the kind of intimacy we have created. So it is only fair, if you ever have questions of me, I will answer.

Grateful for this first acquaintance,
Ashley

July 3, 2018

My close friend, Steve, brought his son, Eddie, for a visit at the jail once. I had been there with Steve when his dark haired little bean had been born. Ed and I used to watch cartoons and go to the park. He was my nephew, little brother, and adopted son all rolled into one. I wanted Ed to remember us watching SpongeBob, playing with video games and matchbox cars. I wanted Ed to remember our adventures at the park. Memories of me tainted by bullet proof glass and institutional scrubs were not the parting gifts I wanted to pass on. When Steve brought Ed in, I was suddenly grateful for the thick glass. I forced aside my anger and looked down to Eddie. He was clutching his father's leg as if his life depended on it. I'll never forget the look on his face. His big watery brown eyes held so much fear and uncertainty. Ed's mouth moved with unasked questions. It was a spear through my middle. All I wanted to do was scoop him up right then. I wanted to tell him that I loved him. I wanted to lie to him, and tell the kid that everything was going to be alright. I was as speechless as he was, for a moment.

"God damn you, Steve!"

I took a steadying breath, "I didn't want him to see me like this!"

I watched helplessly as his world was changed, marred. The visit didn't last much longer, and gratefully, I can't remember the rest. But I remember enough, more than I'd like.

Lelah tried to comfort me. She had such a beautiful heart. Lelah was an amazing woman. There she was trying to give me peace when I had left her none. But that was just how it was with her. Lelah did for others before thinking of herself. I was supposed to be there as a strength, and now I was making her weak. However, ten years is a bond not easily broken. Yet despite having lived almost half of my life with her (at that point), I tried to cut her free. I was a dead weight, and was only going to drag her down with me. I remember barely being able to say the words, choking them out over a phone. Of course, she denied them and in so doing, totally accepted me. I was grateful and touched beyond words. We had a shot. Love had a chance. There was faith, and hope yet still. We were going to see this through together. Lelah and I made plans for "the after" time. I couldn't hold her, I couldn't kiss her and whisper all the things that I thought mattered.

About a year into my sentence, Lelah and I started having contact visits. I had been transferred to prison by then, and visitation was run differently than county jail. Our first hug jolted me solidly, striking me like an open line. We held each other until a supervising officer told us to sit. The separation left me wanting as an addict. We held hands and told each other lies from love. The hour evaporated, and we were pulled apart, again. We saw each other a few more times before the end. I remember our last embrace. Its every sensation is seared to me. I remember how she refused to let me go. Lelah couldn't take her arms from around me. I laughed quietly, "Easy, easy, Sweet Pee Lee. I'll make plenty more hugs for you later." She squeezed me desperately hard before letting me go. I received two more letters from her after that. One mentioned a trip to China with her mom to visit family. The last was several months later, telling me she was pregnant and engaged. I was shattered. I didn't sleep or eat for days. Exhaustion eventually pulled me down into a deep dreamless sleep. I would not do without for long.

I dreamt of her for seven years. When the dreams of her finally stopped, I found myself wanting. I was looking for something that didn't exist on my island. I pined for the soft touch, as much as I did for more primal needs. They say scents are vivid memory triggers. This was a fact I learned to be true. One day as I was looking through pictures and clippings, a bookmark fell out of my folio, scented with her perfume. Slaps to the face have stung less. Yet as a glutton for punishment, I tucked it back away.

Television was a horrible reminder of what was. Everything that mattered was just out of reach. I didn't get visits. I didn't call home. I was on a path that I had been numbly walking for so long that the pain didn't matter anymore. It all registered as background noise. I didn't realize just how much I had changed until someone challenged me.

Her kindness was a subtle magic that wormed its way through my hard shell, and shone its light into darkened corners. Oblivious to my own decay, she made me blink and look about. For years my boss acted as a distant surrogate, encouraging a new growth in me that, in all honesty, probably saved me in more ways than one. I had done without for so long, that I had forgotten what was missing. She encouraged me to write, to vent, cope, and conquer through acts of will. Kindness, and compassion were silent strengths that she gave from example. Had the administration known of her compassion, they would have condemned her as a dangerous heretic. Yet the woman's capacity to care and give freely rekindled a fire in me. Since then it has heated my words and shown me that even amongst all of this, one can make a difference.

My more ravenous appetites sometimes threaten all sense and sensibility. I wish, and lust after, a seemingly unattainable fantasy. I would consume "her" voraciously, completely. All in truth it would take about two minutes.......at first. The fantasy stretches out to lascivious lengths and depraved lusts only satiated after a veritable smorgasbord of sexual feats were accomplished.

Yet I have noticed a reoccurring detail that dies hard. No matter what I do, I just can't shake it. After all is said and done, there is one thing that no fantasy can hold a candle to. It's the quiet moments of shared solitude. The silent words that speak for themselves, sharing the muted moments of an early morning. It's the day's first rays caressing her lips followed by murmured promises of things to be. Somehow, much to my chagrin, I've become a hopeless romantic. This is not something that I searched for, or even wanted originally. Yet who am I to fight the most cliche of battles? After all, no one wins when fighting your own heart.

The reason I wrote such lengthy stories was to "show" you how it felt not to touch. I could "tell" you that I feel like a lost soul drifting about a noisy sea. I could tell you how despite being surrounded by people, I am alone. When one is being tossed about an ocean, all one wants after a time is a drink. I could tell, but I should show.

But if I'm boring you, let me know.

Okay, so I've written more than I anticipated or even cared to dredge up originally. However there is comfort in the digital distance between us. There is safety in confiding in a perfect stranger. After all, the Catholic church has been doing brisk business of the sort for quite some time now. While I believe you are well intentioned, I don't believe any difference will be made here in Virginia. But that's not why I do this, is it. I do this with the hope that some beautiful idealist will grab ahold of my words, and make a difference somewhere, with someone. So as long as you keep asking, I'll keep answering. Maybe, just maybe, the echo of our thoughts will reach receptive ears.

I have to know though, what is it that drives you to do this? What do you hope to accomplish, and what do you actually expect? Do you have any victories? Do enough people actually care beyond morbid curiosity? Will they actually stand tall and bring change and a chance? I have a myriad of questions ranging multiple spectrums. What I want to know most though is what are we to you? Are we a source to be tapped for periodicals? I have been on both sides of disposal. I just want to know what I should expect. Honest answers only. I ain't got time for the bull shit. :)

July 4, 2018

Aubrey,

Once again, your writing feels like an ocean—soft, like I'm floating over a wave, with great depth and the power to move me. Your gift, as you shared, is that you make me feel, not just think. So, even in letters about missing touch, you've managed to touch me.

Thank you for continuing to share you with me. You do not bore me at all.

With gratitude,
Ashley

July 5, 2018

Aubrey,

Now it is my turn to confide in you.

I don't know what brings me to the page, specifically, to this one writing to you. To this project and this book. To choosing to talk with and talk about people who are in prison.

I would like to tell you that it is purely altruistic; humanitarian. But that isn't true. All I can tell you is this: I am guided by a feeling.

As I have gotten older, I have learned to write not from my head, but from my body: I am sensual, I say, because I move, act, create from what I feel, from my senses. I have learned to lead my life from there—from my gut, my soul, my intuition.

So I could tell you a story. I could tell you how, when I was eleven, someone close to me was convicted of a felony, a white collar crime. He never served any jail time but I watched the effects of his actions and the system unfurl together, one consuming the other.

Or I could tell you how, also at eleven, I wrote to then Senator Hillary Clinton about my outrage that many people with felony convictions in this country are stripped of their voting rights. How I was flabbergasted that our democracy disempowered and disenfranchised good people who made mistakes.

Or I could tell you how, one day at the library, not quite fifteen years after my first attempt at political participation, I happened to stumble upon Bryan Stevenson's book *Just Mercy* and how his stories of people, many on death row, knocked me open. It wasn't the stories, though, it was the humanity in them.

But I don't know that any of that matters. I have chosen this project because it has chosen me.

I have chosen this project because I think it was the nectar I was seeking. Because it nourished me, strengthened me, challenged me, asked me to be better and greater and more aware.

Because I feel outrage every time I think of our failures: we're sending people to prison without focussing on change. Because we're neglecting the collective so much that we can't see that we are the cause of our own problem. That we are not caring for all: we are leaving people behind.

Because too many of us are blind to the history of hate that ungirds this country. Arjun Singh Sethi writes, "This country was built on a hate crime." Mass incarceration, drug addiction, abuse, violence, poverty, discrimination are preventable. We need to reckon with our past, open our eyes to our present, in order to transform our future.

We are our own creators. Responsibility rests with no one but us.

This is all to say that every time I get to read a letter from you or have the privilege of responding, in my body, I feel it. I feel called, unable to fulfill the lofty goals of this book and, still, unable not to try.

Let me make a few promises about this project:

1. I am doing this not to be a voyeur or to pretend that I can speak for you or your life. I will publish your words exactly as you've written them, in their fullness, because I refuse to speak over you.

2. By creating this book, I am not a hero or a savior. I am not "giving" you voice. You already have a voice. I am simply collecting it and sharing it. This is a co-creation and I could not do it without you or Taj or anyone else who has been generous enough to share their words.

3. I do not promise to change the Virginia state prison system with this book, but I hope to be that idealist you spoke of—to be part of a growing movement to uncover who we're locking up and its impact. I think it's outrageous that we're continuing to rely on an outmoded 13th amendment that justifies slavery as punishment to throw people behind bars, disappearing them. As you know, we have over 2 million people in prison and jail in this country, and prison's grasp extends beyond them to millions of children and wives and husbands and siblings and parents. In truth, to all of us because what we do to one we do to all. I believe mass incarceration is a human rights crisis that continues right before our eyes; I don't know how we're not more enraged. But maybe there is too much to be enraged by these days. Maybe we are flooded by too much disconnection and information and suffering. For humanity to survive, this must change.

4. Lastly, I think what I have wrestled with most with this project is how much I have gained from it. And I don't mean professionally. I mean personally, spiritually. I have wrestled with how a project that was meant to see and feature you has also seen and celebrated me. How I have learned from each of you in a way that has blown me away. In a way that is life-altering. But I thought about this again this morning: I will not apologize for growing from this project, for receiving. The only thing I should feel guilty about is if I was so disconnected and self-involved that I didn't grow: that I didn't hear those I'm writing to and feel them and listen to them enough to be changed by them. That would be inhuman.

Know that I will do my best to honor you. We cannot keep disposing of our earth and disposing of each other and expect to live long and live well. We have a responsibility to each other. So my only wish, my only victory, would be that I am blessed enough, capable enough not to stumble: I intend to fulfill those promises.

Thank you for calling upon me to answer those questions. No one else has asked.

Sincerely,
Ashley

I Have Waited for You: Letters from Prison

ABOUT THE AUTHOR

Ashley Asti is a writer, speaker, and creator of a grassroots organic beauty and skincare movement. She is the founder of ASHLEY ASTI skincare, a wellness and beauty line committed to preserving the planet and connecting you to the beauty of your soul. Her other book titles include *The Moon and Her Sisters*, a collection of poetry celebrating our spirits, our earth, and our oneness.

CPSIA information can be obtained
at www.ICGtesting.com
Printed in the USA
LVHW021034070219
606725LV00001B/13/P

9 781718 122727